Land Policy

An exploration of the nature of land in society,
the problem of community created land values
and the twin processes of planning and
development.

The Built Environment series

Series Editors:

Michael J. Bruton, *Head of the School of Planning and Landscape, City of Birmingham Polytechnic*

John Ratcliffe, *Principal Lecturer in Estate Management, The Polytechnic of Central London*

The Spirit and Purpose of Planning   Edited by *Michael J. Bruton*

Introduction to Transportation Planning   *Michael J. Bruton*

Introduction to Town and Country Planning   *John Ratcliffe*

Introduction to Regional Planning   *John Glasson*

Introduction to Town Planning Techniques   *Margaret Roberts*

Citizens in Conflict: An Introduction to the Sociology of Town Planning   *James Simmie*

The Dynamics of Urbanism   *Peter F. Smith*

In association with the Open University Press

The Future of Cities   Edited by *Andrew Blowers, Chris Hamnett* and *Philip Sarre*

Man-Made Futures   Edited by *Nigel Cross, David Elliott* and *Robin Roy*

Land Policy

An exploration of the nature of land in society

John Ratcliffe

Principal Lecturer in Estate Management
Polytechnic of Central London

Hutchinson of London

Hutchinson and Co (Publishers) Ltd
3 Fitzroy Square, London W1

London Melbourne Sydney
Auckland Wellington Johannesburg and agencies
throughout the world

First published 1976
© John Ratcliffe 1976

Set in Monotype Times
Printed in Great Britain by The Anchor Press Ltd
and bound by Wm Brendon & Son Ltd, both
of Tiptree, Essex

ISBN 0 09 127070 7 (cased)
      0 09 127071 5 (paper)

Contents

Preface

I venturesomely embarked upon the task of writing a book on Land Policy for two principal reasons. Firstly, to provide a text which sets out the various arguments surrounding what is commonly described as the Land Question, and secondly to explore in an admittedly more pejorative way the perversely conflicting processes of planning and development which collectively determine the nature and performance of the land market.

Since Peter Hall's admirable report of the proceedings of a colloquium on land values held in London in 1965, there has been no single volume, and relatively few sources, that trace the history and examine the concepts of what is commonly called the compensation-betterment problem, placing it at the same time in the general context of the nature of land in society. Chapters 1–5 aim to fill this void.

Chapters 6–8 briefly indulge my own views in respect of the current state of planning and the unhappy relationship that presently prevails with the property development industry. I believe very strongly that certain elements representing all political persuasions within education, government and the professions have foolishly polarized arguments relating to the future functions of what in a mixed economy should be essentially complementary processes. This book is designed as a reaction to this trend, for having critically appraised the twin processes of planning and development in Chapters 6 and 7 respectively, it attempts to outline the possible prospects for partnership in Chapter 8.

The book is primarily aimed at the professions of the built environment – estate managers, architects, planners, quantity surveyors, builders and engineers. It should also be of interest, however, to other social and political scientists who retain an interest in the dilemma surrounding the nature of community created land values and the role and function of the various public and private sector agencies who become involved in the formulation and implementation of land policy.

Preface

Voltaire declared that 'Work banishes those three great evils, boredom, vice and poverty.' Knowing little of the second and too much of the third, I am left to agree with only the first, for I have been exceptionally fortunate in my working environment over the past years, and therefore dedicate this book to my colleagues in the Estate Management Unit at the Polytechnic of Central London for all their help, guidance and most of all friendship.

JOHN RATCLIFFE
June 1976

1 Land in society

The nature and characteristics of land

Rousseau advanced the argument that original sin arose with the first man who saw fit to appropriate land from the rest of the community by delineating his own boundaries with stakes effectively pronouncing 'This is mine!' Such proprietary attitudes have placed land in a special category when it comes to the framing and execution of social policy, for undeniably, as a scarce resource, land possesses certain distinctive characteristics, some in common with other exchangeable commodities, some unique to land. Orthodox economic analysis asserts that land is relatively fixed in supply, although the quantity may be increased by limited and partial reclamation or marginally decreased by flooding and erosion, and the quality improved by efficient land management and the adroit application of capital. In absolute terms, land is considered irreplaceable for no one piece of land is like any other. This notion has material repercussions in assessing the equity of basing compensation upon compulsory acquisition on simple open market values when exact replacement is impossible. It is maintained that there is no cost involved in the creation of land, nor in the long run is it used up; there are thus 'original and indestructible powers of the soil'.[1] Besides being immobile, land is also said to be subject to the law of eventual diminishing returns to scale whereby past a particular point additional inputs of other factors produce successively lower outputs of the final product.

These widely accepted fundamental characteristics of land have, through their currency, become little more than truisms. They represent merely a starting point, for like many truisms they camouflage a number of underlying fallacies. The idea that, to all intents and purposes, land is fixed in supply becomes a rigid and constraining concept when one considers the reclamation projects performed in the Dutch Polders, Guyana, and elsewhere; the ill-fated proposals for a third London airport on Maplin Sands; the prospects offered by farming the continental shelves; the potential afforded by the construction of barrages across the Wash and other estuaries; not to mention the local impact of innumerable mixed development marina schemes; the possible future realization of under-sea cities currently confined to fertile architectural imaginations; and the even more distant development of inter-planetary mineral exploitation. The dogma of indestructibility is thrown into sharper and more immediate relief in an age dominated by pollution and other forms of environmental despoliation. Erosion by excessive prairie farming; pollution by pesticides, industrial effluent and over-fulsome fertilization; increasing subsidence from mining operations: all threaten 'the original and indestructible powers of the soil'. These are necessary statements of the obvious, for what is frequently implied is that land of a certain type for a specific function is limited in supply. Although the supply of land to particular uses is not so inelastic, it is nevertheless apparent that given conditions of long-term economic growth throughout an economy, the relative fixity of supply in conjunction with an escalating demand produces exceptionally inflated prices in comparison with other more adjustable sectors. The lack of homogeneity, paucity of knowledge, and dearth of many buyers and sellers competing at the same time has led to the land market being repeatedly labelled as imperfect. It is not without justification that it has also been described as chaotic, irrational, monopolistic and therefore not amenable to empirical generalization.

One last recognizable characteristic of land, and one of some relevance to strategic planning in particular, is the difficulty encountered in quantification. This relates not only to measurement in terms of area, productive capacity and value, but also refers to the almost insuperable problems involved in calculating the economic consequences of various land policies.

Land and resource allocation

As a factor of production, land is unlike capital, labour and enterprise in that it exists in the natural order of things. Although Marshall was prepossessed with the aspect of fertility because of its special suitability in describing the law of eventual diminishing returns, he emphasized the uniqueness of land in relation to other factors as follows: 'The requisites of production are commonly spoken of as land, labour and capital, those material things which owe their usefulness to human labour being classed under capital, and those which owe nothing to it being classed as land.'[2]

Land is an almost essential ingredient in all forms of human activity and a primary condition of production. Competition for land is rarely due to a mere psychological avarice. The joys of ownership devoid of pecuniary benefit are available to very few. Again Marshall neatly makes the point: 'Land gives man room for his own actions, with the enjoyment of the heat, the air and the rain which nature assigns to that area; and it determines his distance from, and in great measure his relations to, other things and other persons.'[3]

Though frequently overlooked in framing economic policy, it is this pervasive function of land that singles it out from other factors of production and affirms the need for a closer scrutiny of the part it plays in the planning process. Distinguished further from other factors by their heterogeneous nature, individual plots of land can vary one from another in a variety of ways. Most obvious is the divergence in physical quality, such as the fertility or wealth of the soil, the degree of slope, or the proneness to subsidence or flooding. Naturally there are many others. Owing to this distinctive nature and the consequent disparities that arise, certain areas of land are more propitiously employed in particular uses than in others – the *raison d'être* of land-use planning.

Since land, through the media of location, communication and the provision of complementary services, as well as being the basis of agriculture, can be identified as a function of virtually all forms of production, its availability, management and allocation between competing uses is a prime determinant in the economic performance of a community. Despite the current stigma of 'physical determinism' and the professional slight of 'land accountancy' the practice of land-use planning remains an essential, though increasingly under-rated, contribution to the overall stewardship of the built environment. Despite the fact, however, that land is a resource of primary consequence in the economy of any country[4] it is either left out of national aggregates, or included as a homogeneous unit, quantified in superficial measures and at unrealistic linearly accounted values.[5]

In under-developed or developing countries, a different picture emerges. The reallocation or reform of land resources is commonly considered to be an expedient instrument for achieving greater equity and social justice through the redistribution of income as well as a means of creating an economic system designed for increased productivity. As a representation of a particular arrangement of wealth, the existence and nature of land tenure institutions play a large part in shaping the pattern and degree of income distribution – an observation only too apparent when appraising the inequalities that persist among the various sectors of the housing market in the United Kingdom. This does not imply that land tenure institutions exist or exert influence in isolation, for the dimensions and future security of economic opportunities are critically affected by labour, capital and product markets. It does intimate, however, that the degree and form of land distribution and tenure not only exercise considerable sway over the scale and allocation of resources, but also largely determine the mobility of resources between alternative and competing claims. Again the manifest anomalies of the British housing market, and in particular the vagaries of rent control legislation, amply portray the problem.

All too often problems of resource allocation, economic development and planning policy devolve around an evaluation of alternative strategies where the ownership or control of such resources amongst constituent agencies and individuals is 'given', or at least compensated to maintain equivalent status. Apart from political and philosophical extremes, likely in themselves to be unpropitious or impracticable, the range and variety of intermediate land allocation alternatives, together with an assessment of their resultant economic and social repercussions are rarely investigated, except at infrequent and usually ill-timed intervals. This view is succinctly put by Long: 'The question is not, for example, whether a landlord and a tenant each receives the appropriate return for the resources he controls; but rather is it appropriate, from the standpoint of the economic development of the country in question, for the landlord and the tenant to have these particular proportions of the nation's resources under his control.'[6]

The all-pervading importance of land resource allocation and regulation in the direction of national economic policy has been recognized for some considerable time. As evidence of this Marshall averred in the 1920s that: 'A far-seeing statesman will feel a greater responsibility to future generations when legislating as to land than as to other forms of wealth; and that, from the economic and from the ethical point of view, land must everywhere and always be classed as a thing by itself.'[7] The same author later added the proviso that: 'sudden and extreme measures would be inequitable;

and partly, but not solely for that reason they would be unbusiness-like and even foolish.'

As a development of these views, and following more recent economic analysis with its implicit morphological view of capital,[8] it is important to take account of the overriding heterogeneous nature of land already referred to when considering its function and allocation in relation to the formulation of planning policy. It has been contended that the morphological view of capital is particularly suited to an examination of land resources because it is concerned with what capital does, and how it does it, as opposed to a rather abstract analysis of what it is.[9] Each element involved in the process of production has a distinct, integral and related part to play in the overall outcome. An analysis of the twin processes of planning and development as facets in the general spectrum of resource allocation bereft of an examination and understanding of the role of land, is both partial and limited. In this way, the notion of capital as a collective entity within the context of resource allocation, indicating genus not species, is especially relevant to land-use planning where the complementary nature inherent within General Systems Theory postulates that 'everything in the city affects everything else'.

Varying attitudes towards land

The very term 'land' lends itself to a variety of interpretations. Conventional economic thought considers land as a factor of production, in much the same way as labour, capital and enterprise, but with the distinguishing features already discussed. Marshall[10] defined land as: 'the material and the forces which Nature gives freely for man's aid, in land and water, in air, light and heat'.

An all-embracing, if somewhat Arcadian view. To the agriculturalist, putting aside the current adage that the most productive harvest is housing, an area of land is the means of supporting a certain crop, be it vegetable, cereal, arboreal, or animal, for which purposes the soil must possess certain mechanical and chemical qualities. To the lawyer land is the physical dimension to which a variety and collection of rights are attached. Even the dimension is defined by a wider set of parameters than most, as witnessed by the legal maxim that land extends 'up to heaven and down to hell'!

The architect and builder concern themselves with the structural qualities of land in relation to support and drainage; whilst the surveyor and engineer possess a broader-based brief of physical performance. To the developer, land represents potential – the physical medium which permits the co-ordination and manipulation of other factors critical to the investment decision. The majority of urban and regional planners retain an imperfect view of land as the canvas upon which a plan is presented, 'broad brush' or otherwise; as a mosaic requiring conformity and control; as a miscellany of units to be regulated at the right time, in the right place, for the right use by the right people; as the foundations, simple and certain, of the built environment.

To the individual, land can mean privacy and security, to the politician the polemics of partisan philosophy. The list of definitions is almost endless, for land can mean all things to all men.

The creation of land values

As with any other scarce factor of production, the value of land is determined by the interaction of demand and supply, whether overtly in a relatively free market or covertly as latent value in a controlled society. The general payment for the hire of factors of production is commonly known as commercial rent. This is composed of two constituent elements, 'transfer earnings' and 'economic rent' or, as it is otherwise described, 'scarcity value'. Transfer earnings arise because land can be used for more than one purpose; the most productive and profitable purpose being determined by the highest level of transfer earnings and known as the 'opportunity cost' of land. The economic rent is the return for the scarcity value of land over and above its opportunity cost. Since the supply of land is virtually inelastic, the degree of economic rent accruing to the owner of land is strictly a function of demand. In this way economic rent, and therefore a portion of total land value, is fortuitous and unearned. This notion lies at the very kernel of any analysis of land values and their quintessential relationship with planning policy.

The historical development of land value theory from its Ricardian agricultural inception to the differential appraisal of von Thunen (1826), its urban transportation by Hurd (1903), the marginal cost approach of Marshall (1920), the relevance of transportation costs propounded by Haig (1926), through the ecological views of urban structure advanced by Burgess (1925), Hawley (1950) and others, to the more recent and more sophisticated approach adopted by those such as Turvey (1957), Wendt (1958), Wingo (1961), and Hoyt (1960), is well documented elsewhere.[11] Suffice it to say that most of these works ignore both the societal or external nature of economic rent upon individual land holding and the impact upon planning and development. Others, however, veer to a more emotive extreme; Tolstoy, for example, declaimed that: 'Possession of land by people who do not use it is immoral – just like the possession of slaves', and much of Marxist theory is based upon the notion that the economic corruption of society arises from capitalistic expropriation of 'scarcity value'.

To examine these aspects more closely it is first necessary to recapitulate the classical contention that certain areas of land, due to their inherent physical characteristics, are deemed to be worth more than others. The demand for, and therefore the value of, a given piece of land depends, however, on far more than its intrinsic qualities. It depends essentially upon location and accessibility. Following the terminology of Adam Smith, it is the 'value in exchange' rather than the 'value in use' that is important in an assessment of land values, with exchangeable value being derived from scarcity and the application of labour.[12] Given the demand for various land-use activities, the search for the optimum location, and the resultant bidding process take account of the physical proximity of a wide range of services, facilities, markets and complementary enterprises. A range so wide, in fact, that the individual identification of contributory factors is virtually impossible. Such attempts to isolate and quantify the separate effects of these variables as exist, while providing a useful starting point, are as yet naive and unconvincing. The indivisibility of these constituent determinants of value gives rise to the hypothesis that land values are attributable to the whole of society, past and present. And that: 'They [land values] are not so much a tangible reality in themselves but rather a symptom and reflection of uses in land, of what is happening, has happened and is tending to happen to land use.'[13]

In this country it is reasonable to infer that the principal factor directing both the level and, more particularly, the distribution of land values is the administrative and legislative framework that besets the land market because the value of land today depends largely on public policy and is little influenced by any other action on the part of the owner.

Because no direct financial transaction takes place during the creation of these societal values, being 'externalities', the argument is advanced that the total value of the economic rent should therefore vest in the whole of society, not extraneously and fortuitously reside in individual current ownerships which are in no way attributable to their formation, still less entitled to any unearned increment accruing during the period of tenure.

A rather contrary view of the nature of land value is put forward by Denman[14] who is inclined to reject the differentiation between land and other factors of production:

Land in its physical forms, in which proprietary interests are created, is fixed in supply and the limitation affects in some measure what is available on the land market. Growth in population and wealth will intensify the pressure of general demand and cause prices to rise faster and further than they would have done if supply had been more elastic. What is happening in the community at large affects prices on the land market. To this extent we should admit that the community can be said to participate in the establishment of land values.

Thus far, Denman's analysis represents no fundamental departure from the opinion expressed above. He continues, however:

This influence is a common phenomenon operating wherever the general demand is directed to resources, services and special skills limited and inelastic in supply. It is not a fate peculiar to the land market. If the case for communally created land values rests simply on this common-place consequence, it is insubstantial ground for justifying appropriation of land to the community, or the levying of special charges upon it unless the other resources, rent yielding and in short supply, are acquired or charged also.

Naturally, in the course of events it frequently happens that other commodities apart from land do indeed yield an economic rent. Nevertheless, it could be suggested that Denman has ignored one critical factor in his thesis because scarcity value derived, as the term implies, from a shortage in the supply of practically all commodities, including human abilities, invariably draws forth an increase in the supply of that commodity, albeit with different degrees of time-lag. In the field of human skills this might mean the introduction or expansion of training programmes or the personal development of natural aptitudes and the consequent elimination of the economic rent element. Similarly, in the field of raw materials any prospective shortage can usually be countered by substitution; coal gives way to oil, and in time oil is replaced by nuclear and solar energy. An increase in the demand for land in general, however, does not produce significant increases in supply, for that supply is relatively fixed and devoid of substitutes. Perhaps too much importance is attached, however, in seeking to establish the uniqueness or special relationship of land and the formation of economic rent. Though Hudson[15] insisted upon the generality of the occurrence of surplus in contradistinction to either classical rent theory or the labour theory of surplus value, and both Grey[16] and Lerner[17] propounded the ubiquitous nature of surplus long before Denman's criticism, the fact remains that a community created surplus exists. Inevitably the level of land values varies with the level of general prosperity and is thus, in macro-economic terms, a function of inflation, growth and population. Again the individual impact of independent variables upon land values is a problematic calculation as the failure of Milgram[18] in employing surrogate measures of economic conditions to assist identification, and the superficiality of Ellman[19] in the mere taxonometric treatment of policy indicators, demonstrates. Dynamic modelling approaches have proved equally suspect.

At a more local scale, considerable research has been undertaken aimed at establishing individual determinants of land value;[20] most attempting to break down the elements of accessibility. Some, while accepting the relevance of social factors, accentuate and assess the role of transportation improvements as a single index of accessibility.[21] Others, on the other hand, question the overriding emphasis on accessibility and focus attention upon what is euphemistically described as 'neighbourhood quality',[22] when what is really meant is the effect upon values of the proximity of unwanted ethnic or social groups.

All these countervailing views contribute to the conclusion that land values are determined by all aspects of the planning process, economic, social and political, acting in unison. This is the more so in a society subject to rigorous planning control and public direction. Within prevailing statutory and administrative controls it has therefore been maintained that the prime determinant of market value is the existing use of land.[23] Although undeniably a contributory factor, what is perhaps more crucial to present planning policy is the potential value of land, that entity which the Uthwatt Report in 1942 described as 'floating' value. Floating value, by its very nature, is speculative, representing a pure economic rent or surplus. Although land-use zoning helps to fix these floating values, that zoning mechanism must be certain, current and comprehensive to be effective, otherwise it becomes a speculative stimulus in itself; which, it is suggested, has been very much the case ever since 1947.

Land value taxation

Apart from the equitable arguments favouring recoupment of that portion of community-created land value, it is the existence of an economic rent or surplus, unique or otherwise, that renders land an attractive proposition for taxation. Because taxes on marginal transactions disturb optimum conditions of production an ideal neutral tax should be either non-marginal or lump-sum. The most commonly advocated non-marginal taxes are those imposed on economic surplus, of which land is a prime example. A tax is neutral and most efficient if it places the least burden on the person to be taxed and does not interfere with the functioning of the market. In this context it can be argued that among the range of practicable taxes there is none which is so economically 'efficient' as a tax upon land.

The incidence of land taxation can be traced back to 2697 B.C. and the Huang-Ti dynasty in China. Thomas Spence in 1775 described the problems of the 'unearned increment' and published recommendations for the appropriation of the rent from land. Malthus, following Ricardo and encouraged by both Millses, when appointed first professor at the Imperial Service College, induced young colonial administrators to establish a 'land revenue' in India whereby a detailed cadastral survey linked to records of agricultural yields over preceding years was employed to institute a tax imposed at reasonable non-confiscatory levels on surplus. Nevertheless, Indian experience served to illustrate that a land tax is not always unshiftable and that, with the soil of India for the most part being now less productive, the 'original and indestructible powers' may not in fact endure.

Since Henry George advocated a single tax on property rights in land in 1880, arguing that such a tax would be certain in its effect, easily collected, and equitable in its incidence, a wealth of literature on land and property taxation, and the relative merits of each, has materialized. Although George's nineteenth-century evangelicism foundered in England, it was very much more successful in the United States of America, South Africa, Australia and New Zealand, and during the early years of the twentieth century considerable efforts, even in this country, were devoted towards assessing the merits and deficiencies of land value taxation as an alternative to a tax on property.

Having been in existence since the sixteenth century, rates on 'improved' property values have become a familiar form of local taxation, presently accounting for 34 per cent of local government income. In its favour it can be said to be well established, generally accepted, and, at well over £3000 million per annum in England and Wales alone, highly productive. It can be varied according to circumstances and locality, is readily identified with local government areas and is easily administered. At a cost of 2 per cent of yield it is cheap to collect and difficult to evade. In addition, it is a relatively simple task to alter the rate poundage in order to gain an increase in revenue. On the other side of the coin, it has been criticized for not being related to an individual's ability to pay and, while mitigated by social security and rate rebate schemes, the present rating system displays a certain regressive element. Furthermore, beside penalizing improvement, discouraging development, and possessing a degree of inconsistency and inequity by fluctuation through time, the very basis of original valuation is questionable.

Most of the advantages of property taxation through rating apply equally to land value taxation (also called site value and unimproved value taxation). Having, for many years, been successfully employed in a number of countries throughout the world, it can be said to be administratively practicable, although the rate at which it is charged is frequently pitched at an uncontroversial level. By levying a charge on the optimum use of land, it is said to avoid taxing development or improvements, but what appears to be ignored by most writers on the subject is that the tax can be considered an impost, just as punitive, on total improvement and development. Due to assessment on a basis beyond current boundaries, it is also intended to stimulate the unification of multi-various interests in accordance with prevailing proposals, something which rarely happens in practice. Furthermore, in imposing a liability related to hypothetical developed value, landowners are encouraged to release or develop vacant sites. From experience gained in Australia and South Africa, land value taxation is said to encourage not only development but good development; although it appears that quality is often equated with quantity. Perhaps the most attractive characteristic with which a system of land value taxation is endowed is that relating to social justice, for it can be said that the fundamental purpose of land value taxation is the apprehension of capital gains.

The implementation of an effective land value taxation policy is, however, fraught with difficulties as the dilatory introduction in Jamaica aptly demonstrates. The taxation base requires detailed land-use zoning and continuitive cadastral survey. There is the inherent problem of measuring base site value, although the use of a standard rate has been suggested as a means of ameliorating this enigma. The designation of optimum use probably presents the most Herculean task of all if the system is truly to be used as a proper planning tool, a development incentive and an economic stimulus, rather than just a pragmatic method of revenue collection. Inevitably the fixed, certain and rigid nature of the cartographic base for taxation purposes is destined to be contrary to the spirit and purpose of strategic planning. The horrendous valuation and revaluation procedures, the eventual lack of cleared-site comparables in developed areas leading to the use of arbitrary ratios, the economic and political delicacy regarding exemptions, and the ever-present dilemma that emerges with any rating system whereby rich areas grow richer, and that where values are low rates are inordinately high, all militate against a smooth and expeditious introduction.

Despite these forebodings regarding the introduction of some kind of site value tax or rate, there can be little doubt that land taxation, whether it be based on property, bare sites, development value or capital gains, is an important factor in planning policy. It may encourage or discourage monopoly, abet or restrict socially undesirable or aesthetically displeasing speculation. It can recapture for the community those values brought about by publicly instituted improvements. Likewise, it can channel into public coffers some of the increased values due to demographic changes. It can create a milieu which encourages or discourages economically and socially significant land uses, stimulating or stifling competition in the purchase and sale of property.[24] Nearly every tax affects land values. In this country, the system of taxation actively discriminates against the private rented sector of the housing market and in favour of owner-occupation. Moreover, despite a lack of evidence, the absence of a tax on vacant land is currently said to encourage land hoarding, which, if true, even the form of a proposed Development Land Tax will do little to alleviate. In many European countries such as Holland, Austria, Greece, Ireland, Italy, Portugal and Spain, the imposition of 'transfer-taxes' ranging from 4 per cent to 15 per cent presents a serious impediment to both property and labour markets, reducing exchange and mobility alike. Another application is the use made of preferential taxes in furthering regional development policies.

Similarly, progressive taxation such as that in Austria, Belgium,

Finland, France and Norway is used to discourage large land-holdings, and throughout Europe capital gains taxes of varying types and orders are levied consequent to such acts as the removal of prior zoning regulations and the sale of improved land. In this way, taxation can be seen to be a valuable, if somewhat neglected, instrument of planning policy. More than this, it can be argued that present fiscal policy and land-use planning are pulling in opposite directions with disastrous effects upon what might be best described as national estate management, for it can be maintained that a fiscal policy to complement national estate management cannot be drawn up without knowledge of the facts relating to the land market.

Land tenure

Systems of land tenure embody those legal, contractual or customary arrangements whereby individuals or organizations gain access to economic or social opportunities through land. The precise form of tenure is constituted by the rules and procedures which govern the rights and responsibilities of both individuals and groups in the use and control over the basic resource of land.[25]

In addition, it is imperative to recognize, as previously intimated, that the various institutions of land tenure are instrumental in shaping the pattern of income distribution within a community. Land, without the dimension of tenure, is a meaningless concept. In using the very expressions 'land' and 'land tenure', one is more usually concerned with the complicated collection of rights to use space. This 'bundle of rights' includes the rights of access, of light and air, of occupation and development, and of the alienation or abridgement of the many privileges associated with a given terrestrial site, both above and below it.

In accentuating the importance of land as a 'fundamental unit' Denman and Prodano[26] state that: 'these two elements, the run of property rights and the area of physical land to which they pertain together constitute the decision-making unit which is fundamental to all positive decisions about land use and which is referred to as the "proprietary land unit".'

These rights and privileges in property are girdled around by a number of important restrictions: restrictions imposed by statute, by the physical contiguity or proximity of one unit of land to another, and by the existence of inferior and superior interests in the same unit of land. In outlining these regulatory conditions, the point has been made that in a sophisticated and civilized society no individual can hold an absolute proprietary interest in land. The collection or run of property rights is always an abstraction from absolute power.[27]

To facilitate analysis a number of basic rights relating to the ownership of land can be identified. Firstly, a *surface right* which permits a landowner to enjoy the current use of his land. Even this right, however, can only be exercised within the limits of the legal code and with the uncertainties of public acquisition. Secondly, a *productive right*, which allows an owner to make a profit from the current use of his land. This privilege is naturally the subject of taxation, and has been ever since the imposition of Danegeld based upon acreage by Ethelred the Unready. Thirdly, a *development right*, allowing the owner to improve his property, which has been severely circumscribed by successive bouts of planning legislation. Fourthly, a *pecuniary right*, whereby a landowner benefits financially from development value both actual and anticipated. It is this right which has proved so politically contentious over the years, and is examined in very much greater detail later. Fifthly, a *restrictive right*, effectively granting the right not to develop, and which, despite proposals regarding the public ownership of land, and the penalties of site value taxation if it were introduced, still remains largely intact. Sixthly, a *disposal right*, allowing an owner to sell or will his land; and currently this last right is constantly being eroded by taxation. In this way, absolute ownership of land becomes almost an illusion, for even a 'fee simple absolute in possession', the most complete form of land tenure, is notionally subservient to control by the Crown. Nevertheless, while discounting Royal prerogative and the presence of planning control, freehold tenure still does not imply total and independent authority over all possible uses and consequent values of land because of the mutual determination of function among multi-various ownerships. What freehold does confer, however, in this simplified situation, is security of tenure, for, in the absence of public powers of compulsory acquisition, freehold is unassailable. Nevertheless, where powers of compulsory purchase are operative, and one can identify in our own code something like sixty different occasions, the status of freehold is immediately debased, for, despite the award of compensation, the sanctity of security of tenure is breached. With the introduction of, and adherence to, a formal system of planning control, the status of freehold tenure becomes even more shaky, for the very nature of planning and intervention involves a subjugation of the unbridled interests of the individual to the interests of the community in circumstances where the intentions of the individual threaten to endanger the general good.

An essential ingredient in the development process, and thus in the implementation of planning policy, is the creation and transferability of a number of property rights attached to the same piece of land. This potential has not escaped the British property developer whose special expertise in the management of property portfolios is now a byword throughout Western Europe. An understanding of the nature and relevance of tenure institutions, the workings of the property market, and the stimulation of appropriate development does, however, appear to evade the perception of the planner. Planning, after all, is intended to perform a positive as well as negative function.

Land and the property market

The earlier description of land as being original and indestructible, costless in creation, relatively fixed in supply, and immobile, becomes a much more limited notion when attempting to examine the nature and value of property and the impact upon planning policy and development.

Although the total supply of land in this country might be virtually fixed, this is manifestly not the case when one considers the supply of land for urban property development. Rural land may change to urban use, urban land may be transferred from one use to another, the use of land for a particular activity may be intensified, and land may change from private to public ownership. Such changes may transpire through the activities of the market, or through public intervention, or even by a combination of both private and public actions.

A common consensus exists that the value of land in a free market reflects an 'exchange worth'. As a medium of exchange, the property market, however, does not exist as a corporate entity. Unlike most commodity markets it lacks a central agency or set of agencies. In this way it is informal, decentralized, and non-institutional; being simply the abstract aggregation of all property transactions taking place throughout the country. Moreover, as shown in the previous section, the market does not deal in land or buildings as such but rather in the rights or interests in, on, over or under land. It is these rights and interests which constitute the commodity 'property', and their scarcity which creates the necessity for a market to provide a rationing device allocating them between competing claims.

In common with all real world markets, the property market does not match up to the economists' criteria for conditions of perfect competition. Incomplete knowledge, a certain monopolistic element inherent in land ownership, the unique nature of individual properties, the durability of dwellings and their immobility, the indivisibility of the majority of interests in property, the dilatory nature of development and redevelopment processes, the implications of government intervention at both central and local levels, and the high costs of management and conveyance all conspire to produce highly imperfect market conditions.

Besides being complex in the form of its imperfection, it is also diverse in the range of its activities. It possesses national, regional and local characteristics, and even these are but a convenient generalization for collectively describing a group of separate, albeit interacting, sub-markets concerned with different types of property. Nevertheless, the investment implications implicit throughout the property market must not be isolated from those of the general investment market. Prospective investors, in appraising alternative opportunities, will assess the security that any investment affords to capital, the probability of secure and regular income, the expectation of future income or capital growth, the liquidity rating of the investment, and the management expense involved in ownership. The respective degrees of risk and uncertainty will naturally be reflected in the rate of return and, by capitalization, in the value. Generally speaking, of course, the greater the risk the higher the return required. Property investment yields do not, however, exist in a vacuum. There is firstly an inter-relationship between yields from different types of property, whether categorized by the nature of the interest or the nature of the use. Secondly, there is a relationship between property yields and all other non-property investment opportunities. This latter consideration cannot be over-emphasized since it is unusual, not to mention unwise, for a prospective investor to examine one particular type of investment in isolation. The level of urban property values and consequently the development incentive is thus partly a function of the general investment market. Though widely recognized in economic analysis and inherent in financial appraisal these factors are frequently neglected in the framing of planning policy.

The conflict of land law and statutory planning

The tradition of private ownership of land subsisting in this country, common to most liberal democracies, with its assorted notions of private rights protected by the law, belongs irreconcilably to an age when scant regard was paid to land as a scarce national resource to be deployed in a manner amenable to the interests of the community as a whole. These inherited notions, in so far as they still persist, are in direct conflict with the aims of national estate management. Traditional land law and contemporary planning legislation appear as disconnected spheres of interest. Land law, consolidated in 1919, re-enacted and implemented in 1925, remains firmly rooted in its common law antecedents. Although many of the intricacies and terminology of its feudal heritage have been removed, the basic feudal concepts regarding proprietary interests endure.[28] As Charles Dickens on land law derisively declaimed:

Nothing but a mine below it on a busy day in term-time, with all its records, rules and precedents collected in it, and every functionary belonging to it also, high and low, upward and downward, from its son the Accountant General to its father the Devil, and the whole blown to atoms with ten thousand hundredweight of gunpowder would reform it in the least.

Whereas the law relating to the land expresses the traditional rights, powers and privileges of individuals over land, planning law has very different origins. Essentially, it has developed, since its approximate inception in the Public Health Act of 1875, as a field of socially conscious legislation progressively increasing the power of community interests over private ones. It attempts to personify the statutory will of that community in the realization of its needs, frequently in the face of the established rights of individuals. The very existence of planning law can be said to represent the conflict between public interest and the private ownership of land. Moreover, notwithstanding the circumstances whereby the planning profession have come to regard the current codes of compulsory purchase, compensation and domain, together with the prevailing market in land and its inherent inflated prices, spiralling costs, and speculative gains, as normal and acceptable components of the framework within which to operate, it does not preclude deliberation regarding a possible reconstruction of the framework. If the legislation of compromise is burdensome to planning, then the nature of the conflicting notions should be examined and the anachronistic ones abandoned, so that the law can be rephrased in simpler terms,[29] for, following Hargreaves,[30] 'land is a valuable asset, the use of which must be controlled in the public interest, and land law is no longer solely a matter of the extent of an individual's rights in his land', which, in turn, echoes Jeremy Bentham who proclaimed over a century ago that: 'property rights, like other rights, are to be tested by their effects on the public good or well-being'.[31]

References

1 D. Ricardo, *On the Principles of Political Economy and Taxation*, 1817.
2 A. Marshall, *Principles of Economics*, Macmillan, 1920.
3 *ibid.*
4 D. Denman and S. Prodano, *Land Use*, Allen and Unwin, 1972.
5 A. Schonfield, *Modern Capitalism*, Oxford University Press, 1965.
6 E. Long, 'Some Theoretical Issues in Economic Development', *Journal of Farm Economics*, vol. 34, 1962.
7 Marshall, *op. cit.*
8 Denman and Prodano, *op. cit.*
9 *ibid.*
10 Marshall, *op. cit.*
11 W. Alonso, *Location and Land Use*, Harvard University Press, 1964.
12 Ricardo, *op. cit.*
13 N. Lichfield, 'Land Nationalisation', *Land Values*, P. Hall (Ed.), Sweet and Maxwell, 1965.
14 D. Denman, *New Horizons in Land and Property Values*, RICS, 1964.
15 J. Hudson, *Economics of Distribution*, Macmillan, New York, 1900.
16 A. Grey, 'Urban Renewal and Taxation', *Land and Building Taxes*, A. Becker (Ed.), TRED, 1969.
17 A. Lerner, *The Economics of Control*, Macmillan, New York, 1944.
18 G. Milgram, *The City Expands*, University of Pennsylvania, 1967.
19 P. Ellman, quoted in Drewett, R. 'Land Values and Urban Growth', *Regional Forecasting*, M. Chisholm (Ed.), Butterworth, 1971.
20 See for example:
   P. Downing, 'Estimating Residential Land Value by Multi-Variate Analysis', *The Assessment of Land Value*, D. Holland (Ed.), TRED, 1971.
   P. Wendt, 'Economic Growth and Land Values', *Appraisal Journal*, July, 1958.
   F. Adams and G. Milgram, 'The Time Path of Underdeveloped Land

Prices During Urbanisation', Discussion Paper 24, University of Pennsylvania, 1966.

S. Weise, T. Donnelly and E. Kaiser, *Land Value and Land Development Influence Factors*, University of Carolina, 1967.

M. Yeates, 'The Effect of Zoning on Land Values in American Cities', *Essays in Geography*, J. Whitton and P. Wood (Eds), Austin Miller, 1965.

S. Cymanski, 'Effects of Public Investment on Urban Land Values', *Journal of the American Institute of Planners*, vol. 32, 1966.

21 A. Mohring, 'Land Values and Measurement of Highway Benefits', *Journal of Political Economy*, vol. 69, 1961.

22 M. Stegman, 'Accessibility Models and Residential Location', *Journal of the American Institute of Planners*, vol. 35, 1969.

23 R. Thomas, 'Land Values and Accessibility', *The City as an Economic System*, The Open University, 1973.

24 Housing and Urban Development Department, *Urban Land Policy – Selected Aspects of European Experience*, HUD-94-SF, 1969.

25 P. Dorner, *Land Reform and Economic Development*, Penguin, 1972.

26 Denman and Prodano, *op. cit.*

27 *ibid.*

28 P. Campbell, unpublished diploma thesis on land nationalization, UCL, 1969.

29 *ibido*

30 A. Hargreaves, *An Introduction to the Principles of Land Law*, Sweet and Maxwell, 1936.

31 Quoted in M. Ginsberg (Ed.), *Law and Opinion in England in the Twentieth Century*, Stevens, 1959.

2 Community created land values

Planning and the redistribution of values

The nature of statutory planning effectively implies a wholesale redistribution of land values, and therefore wealth, throughout the community. This can either occur overtly by the allocation of land for specific purposes, or less directly by broad strategic zoning, alterations in accessibility, the provision of public services and utilities, enhanced environmental amenity, or by general measures aimed at protection and control. In any examination of the financial implications of planning policy a picture emerges of a constantly changing pattern and quantum of values, fluctuating in both absolute and relative terms, determined by a variety of separate but interacting forces. Some, such as the grant of increased planning permission, are readily identified, measured and accountable; others, such as general demographic changes, are less immediately recognized or registrable. The problem of accurately ascribing individual components of total value to particular actions or agencies is one that has continued to exercise the minds of land economists and political philosophers alike. This precise pursuance of abstract polemics is greatly overrated when so little empirical evidence is available to assist in the analysis.

In an attempt to discover a lasting and comprehensive solution to the question of land values and land-use planning, it has been held that: 'From the point of view of planning the ideal is that the best plans should be prepared unhampered by financial considerations.'[1]

Perhaps the propitious preparation of plans is enhanced by this disregard of financial repercussions, but such insouciance is at least imprudent if not irresponsible in ensuring viability and performance in implementation. It is an imperative duty placed upon the planning profession that they should comprehend the impact of the financial forces they unleash and predict the inevitable repercussions flowing from their decisions. In this way, it is not only possible to safeguard the interests of peculiarly imperilled sections of society but also to recoup some of the dividends of community action.

It can be argued that intervention in the market mechanism and the consequent redistribution of land values by way of the planning process is only justified if an overall benefit to the community results. Employing the terminology of welfare economics the criterion for assessing planning performances should be that implied by a Kaldor-Hicks optimum whereby the sum of those made better-off should exceed the sum of those made worse-off, as opposed to a Pareto optimum which merely stipulates that nobody should be made worse-off. Thus, a societal surplus is created. However, in deciding how those who have lost by the imposition of planning decisions should be compensated by those who have gained, the whole thorny problem of distributional equity arises. This opens up much wider and more intractable issues regarding the very function and philosophy of planning; issues concerning the efficiency as opposed to the redistributional function of planning but beyond the restricted scope of this text. It is sufficient to state that despite successive attempts to establish a value-free theory of planning, value judgements inevitably intrude. There are many who believe that it is the responsibility of government acting through the medium of those professions involved in social, environmental and physical planning continually to redistribute the resources and the power generated in the market-orientated mixed economy that prevails towards the deprived, the disadvantaged, and the less powerful groups in society. While this clearly represents a marked political viewpoint, the argument runs that present planning practice is actually regressive,[2] disequilibrating as between sectors,[3] and manifestly inequitable in many of its major decisions.[4] These criticisms are relevant to this study in that they all cite the disparities of income distribution occasioned by planning practice as being reflected in terms of the value of property rights, thereby underlining the vexed nature and all-pervasive importance of the land question.

The argument can also be advanced that planning has failed to realize its original aims because the efforts of planners have not only been dissipated but have also been condemned by their inadequate understanding of the social and economic systems that they attempt to regulate.[5] Again, it bears repetition to emphasize that a much neglected, though integral aspect of those systems is the customary, legal, social, and financial elements, both public and private, that underpin the land market.

The controversial problem of betterment and worsenment

The financial reconciliation of public intervention into market mechanisms for allocating scarce resources in an effort to maximize economic welfare has remained as a burning issue throughout a century distinguished by successive, though largely abortive, attempts to find a solution. To clarify the terminology employed, *betterment* is the fortuitous increase in the value of land, previously described as the economic rent, scarcity value, or unearned increment, which accrues to the owner of land on account of the actions of others, often public authorities. On the other hand, *worsenment* is the term used to describe a decrease in value due to the actions of others. On those occasions when payment is made to mitigate the hardship of such loss, it is known as *compensation*.

In similar vein, it is worth attempting to define the various components of land value which are created as a result of community action of one kind or another. The philosophy that underlies the dissident concept of collecting betterment stems from the notion that being a community created value it is, as far as the individual is concerned, random and extrinsic, moreover, large portions of it must be rendered up to ensure adequate measures of compensation are made available to alleviate the incidence of worsenment. The philosophic and political arguments, though lengthy and tortuous, are cogently summarized in Palgrave's *Dictionary of Political Economy*[6] where the recovery of betterment is defended as follows:

that persons benefited by public expenditure should contribute to such expenditure to the extent of the increased value of their property, and this not only if the improvement effected by the local authority was carried out for the purposes of conferring a benefit on such property, but also if the resulting benefit was purely accidental, the expenditure having been undertaken for a totally different purpose.

Even though it is common practice to equate the notion of betterment with that of worsenment, the conceptual relationship is not matched by an exact quantitative relationship. The respective societal induced changes in land value do not cancel out, for if this were so it would not merely reflect even the Pareto optimum mentioned previously where nobody was worse-off, but a static, impotent equilibrium where society at large was not better-off.

There would be no economic function for intervention, no productive purpose in planning, and the sole reason for regulation and control of market forces and subsequent redistribution of income would be welfare-orientated. Justifiable enough in itself, perhaps, but a restriction to political objectives and a disregard of efficiency criteria. If the two are to be harmonized, which is normally the intention of government in a mixed economy, then the accumulation of betterment should outweigh the incidence of worsenment. In this way, it should theoretically be possible to make total reparation for community action.

Betterment

The practice of planning emerged in response to the realization that the development process imposes a wider array of costs and benefits upon society at large than those borne by the individual landowner. The attention of planning has, for far too long, been focussed upon the cost side of the social balance sheet with the aim of internalizing detrimental 'spillover' effects. Concern on the benefit side has notionally been confined to expediting and facilitating the functioning of free market processes, a laudable enough objective in a mixed economy so long as the control mechanism is effective and not jeopardized by an inappropriate financial base or negated by professional inadequacy.

With increasing urbanization and the expansion of tertiary services over the last twenty years, combined with the boom in demand for leisure facilities, and, until recently, the general growth in the level of economic activity, there has been a consequent rise in aggregate demand which in turn has been reflected in soaring land and property values. It is the planning powers exercised by constituent local authorities that are the prime determinant in physically apportioning these values. As a result of the extremely high level of demand which endured in the commercial and residential sectors, and the lack of any system for recouping the inherent scarcity values, developers became accustomed to excessive, some might say extortionate, returns. In addition to which, the anachronistic method of raising local government revenue through rating, combined with the paucity of development expertise available to local authorities produced a poor and imbalanced negotiating relationship between the planning and development processes. It is not as if all these proceeds from speculation in property development were being channelled back into the national economy priming further investment and development. A large, and now growing, proportion of such profits are held and reinvested abroad.

This pattern of speculation in the property market is self-generating. The massive fluctuation in profit levels breeds uncertainty in investment which requires successively higher returns in order to call forth further funds. In a demand-orientated market the public determination of land use, linked with private control of land ownership, winds the inflationary and speculative spiral tighter and tighter. The underlying forces of risk, uncertainty and high returns are heightened by flexible planning policies. Flexible planning policies can in turn be taken to be synonymous with strategic planning policies. Strategic planning is thought to be not just desirable but essential in formulating a framework for effective social and economic action. As will be argued in Chapter 6, however, without a realistic and efficient system of detailed and current local plans underpinning the strategic framework, defining the direction of future development, stimulating yet stabilizing the agencies of development 'at play' in the market, assisting the overall implementation of planning policy, the present position pertaining to planning and development becomes both paradoxical and intractable.

The skilful exercise of the existing powers available to local authorities relating to compulsory purchase and joint development might have proved successful but the odds were heavily stacked against them and despite a large number of highly successful partnership schemes the sorry saga of opportunities forgone is formidable. With government at all levels intending to embark upon increased public sector development, with all the ensuing social and economic repercussions, it would seem prudent to make adequate provision for collecting some portion of the unearned increment produced by such forms of societal action. If, for no other reason, betterment should be recouped so that the community can at last afford to rectify the monstrous omissions in our code governing compensation for worsenment. This argument, with its implied criticism, is not simply a subjective political reaction to prevailing disparities in the distribution of wealth, it relates to the efficiency of intervention and the effectiveness of planning policy, for if environmental planning is to be at all viable it needs to possess a substantial measure of self-sufficiency and regeneration.

By this stage, therefore, most of the principal motives favouring the recovery of betterment have already been introduced, but to recapitulate, they are that firstly the widespread increase in land values emerges as a result of general social and economic activity; it is not attributable to the actions of individual owners of land. These enhanced values should, therefore, not accrue to private landowners but be collected by the community at large. Secondly, the nature of planning and the practice of public authorities inevitably leads to an extensive redistribution of wealth throughout society and of necessity this wealth is unevenly and fortuitously spread, benefiting some but not others. A solution aimed at mitigating the harshness and inequity of this disparate distribution should be sought. Thirdly, it is thus necessary to recoup betterment in order to make payments alleviating worsenment. Fourthly, the excessive speculation within the land market inherent in inflationary circumstances is exacerbated in the absence of a tax on betterment. Unchecked and unclaimed, these inflationary and speculative spirals place a heavy burden upon local authorities, and accordingly ratepayers, in the purchase of land for public development. Fifthly, funds eventually become available for publicly sponsored development projects thus permitting the internalizing of future potential betterment. And, finally, through remuneration, comprehensive planning is facilitated and the tight grip of private development agencies is loosened.

Once the principle of betterment collection is established, it is necessary to decide the rate at which it is levied. Many varying levels have been mooted or practised. The Liberal government led by Lloyd George introduced separate and selective taxes on a range of different circumstances. The Uthwatt Quinquennial Scheme suggested 75 per cent, the Town and Country Planning Act 1947 implemented a 100 per cent charge on development value, the recent Land Commission levied betterment at 40 per cent with a view to increasing it to 45 per cent then 50 per cent and possibly higher, Capital Gains Tax has been imposed at 30 per cent, Development Gains Tax even higher, and proportions such as $33\frac{1}{3}$ per cent, 60 per cent and now $66\frac{2}{3}$ per cent and 80 per cent have all been advocated at one time or another.

While it is theoretically sound to recoup total betterment, it has certain obvious practical difficulties. The immediate imposition of 100 per cent levy is said to stultify the land market and discourage essential investment and development. Although the performance of the 1947 Act appears to support this claim, it is frequently forgotten that other post-war exigencies of materials, construction and capital exercised a debilitating effect upon development. Nevertheless,

B

it is naturally unwise to ignore or deny evidence presented by past experience despite forceful arguments favouring full recoupment unless the functioning of free market processes is to be radically adjusted or abandoned entirely.

Worsenment

Thus far, attention has been focussed upon the betterment side of the coin, and it could be maintained that a disproportionate degree of effort in practice has been so concentrated. The other side reveals the frequent, and much reported, deleterious impact of planning schemes upon individual land holdings. The virulent consequences of urban motorway programmes over the last couple of decades have highlighted the incidence of worsenment through planning activities. The magnitude of these policies was amply portrayed by Thomson[7] who estimated in 1970 that 250000 people would live within 200 yards of the late, but not lamented, Ringway I London Motorway Box, and suffer the inevitable repercussions. This urban aberration was emphasized at the time by the almost total depreciation effected in the much publicized circumstances surrounding the occupants and owners of Acklam Road who were dominated and degraded by the elevated omnipresence of Westway. A case which also exemplifies the anomaly that the intrusion of privacy and destruction of environmental amenity, propagated through the media of noise, fumes, vibration and visual pollution, often affects those who have not tangibly lost property to a greater extent than those who have. These gross inadequacies of our current compensation code are reinforced by recent proposals relating to air transport. The much vilified Roskill Commission, in making their recommendation for a site for the Third London Airport, recognized that such a decision brought with it immense problems of compensation. Despite the present abandonment of the scheme, paragraph 7.2 of the Commission's report, identifying a major omission in our law relating to compensation for worsenment, deserves quotation: 'The present compensation laws help only those whose homes have been expropriated. Those whose homes are rendered almost uninhabitable by noise receive no help save in some cases a contribution towards partial soundproofing.'

Many examples of the damaging results of the redistribution of land and property values through the incidence of public planning and development can be discerned. Some are obvious, such as the proximity to detracting land uses which exercise a depreciating effect on neighbouring property, the refusal or revocation of planning permission, the instant withdrawal of certain services and facilities, or the allocation of a particular plot on a statutory plan for public development purposes. Others are less pronounced, such as the gradual rundown of public services, a planned decline in local economic activity, the intimation of inclusion for compulsory acquisition on a non-statutory plan, or the fostering of growth or deflection of development elsewhere. A novel, yet evident factor, is the form of publicly sponsored worsenment and social depreciation more familiarly encountered in the field of welfare economics and described as the 'perverse' effect whereby the provision, via the planning mechanism, of a public facility intended to benefit the less privileged produces entirely the opposite result. The creation of a new health or recreation centre, or the opening of a new school, might so change the general attraction of an area or neighbourhood, for example, that the pressure of increased demand on the part of those willing and able to pay for proximity to the new facility might, over time, force out the less able and willing, for whom it was originally designed, to cheaper accommodation elsewhere. This manifestation does not easily fit into the generally accepted concept of worsenment, or immediately lend itself to inclusion in the overall balance sheet of social accounts; nevertheless it is a cost incurred as the recent history of property values and occupancy in Improvement Areas has demonstrated.

Although the use of cost benefit analysis and other equally 'sophisticated' evaluation techniques are employed in scrutinizing and guiding planning decisions regarding the siting of public improvements and the formulation of policy, implying that the social cost of the loss of amenity is at least recognized, it does not compensate the landowners for the loss they suffer.

Despite the limited, though welcome, proposals contained in the Land Compensation Act 1973, there remains scant provision for compensation for injurious affection where no land is taken from an owner as part of a planning scheme. Even where compensation is payable, either upon compulsory acquisition or for injurious affection, the principle of 'equivalence', together with restricted disturbance payments, is probably inadequate particularly in times of excessive inflation.

The perennial problem of 'planning blight' whereby land and property values can effectively be sterilized over a long period of time looms large in the list of public grievances voiced against the practice of physical land-use planning, and the situation regarding wide-scale worsenment in relation to both the planning and development processes has taken on a fresh complexion over the last few years with the growing questioning of the way in which alternative plans are generated and planning policies decided. The scepticism with which planning is increasingly viewed has given rise to vigorous demands for a wider exposure and fuller discussion by the public, on whose behalf the plans are supposedly prepared. The Committee on Public Participation under the late Arthur Skeffington, reporting in 1969, expressed the essential nature of the difficulties which arise from the disclosure, amplification and public debate of planning policy in paragraph 212:

There is a conflict between, on the one hand, the desirability of giving full publicity at an early stage to proposals the planning authority are considering, so as to stimulate informed public discussion and, on the other hand, the need to avoid causing hardship to individuals by the casting of blight over land or property which may not be acquired for many years or, indeed, at all.

A proposition put more pithily by Samuels: 'Participation breeds blight; non-participation minimises blight.'[8]

Despite recent reservations regarding methodology, the assured and inevitable growth of public participation, and the implicit intensification of the incidence of worsenment, demands a solution. If the dilemma is soluble at all, it will only be so within the framework of adequate solutions to the entire betterment-worsenment dichotomy, for the very fact that the prospect of compulsory purchase produces a depreciation in property values itself suggests that the level of compensation is generally inadequate. In these circumstances, the conclusion reached by the Skeffington Committee that 'There is no ready answer to the problem and we can do little more than draw attention to it and express the hope that in drawing up material for publicity and participation, planning authorities will take great care to avoid unnecessary blight on properties or anxiety to those who may be affected' represents an optimism bordering upon naivety. Without reforms encompassing a satisfactory code for the payment of worsenment, and in the absence of any indication of the present prepossession of public concern moving away from the preservation of personal vested interest towards a more dispassionate appraisal of alternative strategies in the light of broader social goals, the appropriateness of public participation must be seriously placed in question.

Again, it is possible to summarize the arguments for making some form of reparation for the incidence of worsenment. Firstly, it is manifestly unjust to collect betterment without paying compensation for worsenment. Secondly, with increased public investment, planning and development the depreciating effect of community directed action is more ruinous and diffused than ever before. Thirdly, the individual citizen should not personally have to bear the brunt of works carried out in the wider public interest. Fourthly, individual loss occasioned by public action may represent a high proportion of personal wealth accumulated with great effort over a long period of time. Fifthly, the payment of worsenment on the part of public authorities might well provide a stimulus for a closer consideration of the full repercussions consequent upon their proposals, thus leading to improved decision-making. And finally, compensation for worsenment would reduce hostility to planning proposals, and therefore public participation.

Whilst the majority of informed opinion right across the political spectrum now accept the need to garner some portion of betterment or development value, a number of arguments are commonly advanced against a system of broader based worsenment payments. Samuels[9] presents a succinct digest of these criticisms:

1 It would cost hundreds of millions of pounds and slow down desirable public works.
2 There is an inherent risk of gains and losses in a capitalist system.
3 An authority should not be forced to acquire land it cannot use.
4 Better design techniques are lessening the impact of worsenment.
5 The refusal of planning permission is not compensated.

Taking these points in turn, it is undeniable that substantial claims for compensation would add to the relative cost of planning. It is not an absolute increase, however, but merely public authorities shouldering the costs that would otherwise have been borne by the numerous individuals and organizations whose property was adversely affected by the planning scheme in question. As previously intimated, the additional accountability of authorities for worsenment might provide a more realistic basis of financial fact upon which to judge planning policy. The comment regarding the factor of chance prevailing in any capitalist system raises fundamental issues relating to the whole nature of society and its economic organization which are beyond the terms of this study. Nevertheless, it is extremely doubtful whether or not, in a mixed economy with substantial government intervention at all scales of activity, the random element of benefits and costs can be countenanced with such complacency. As to local authorities reluctantly being forced to acquire land, if this should actually occur, and the land is rendered useless as a direct result of public action, then there could be no better result than for the authority to so purchase, bearing the blight outright. Equally, it is with great trepidation that one views the responsibilities outlined in current legislation regarding the public ownership of land. The proposition that advanced techniques in design are available and already alleviating the imposition of worsement is unfortunately not borne out by fact, unless it merely refers to such partial cures as soundproofing. Quite the contrary case can be advanced, for as society becomes more 'sophisticated', the intrusion into privacy, particularly that perpetrated by transport improvements, becomes increasingly intolerable. Samuels' final criticism that refusal of planning permission does not attract compensation is not in itself a valid argument against compensation for worsement, for it neglects the basic premise that the right to develop, and the subsequent values obtaining, represent the very nature of betterment and are community created and claimed. Probably the most weighty argument that can be brought against the introduction of a comprehensive code for assessing and compensating worsement, one strangely side-stepped by Samuels, is that of administrative complexity and cost. This aspect will be returned to in a subsequent examination of alternative strategies.

References

1 A. Uthwatt (Chairman), *Expert Committee on Compensation and Betterment*, Cmnd. 6386, HMSO, 1942.

2 J. Simmie, 'Physical Planning and Social Policy', *Town Planning Institute Journal*, vol. 57, 1971.

3 D. Harvey, 'Social Processes, Spatial Form and the Redistribution of Real Income in an Urban System', *Regional Forecasting*, M. Chisholm (Ed.), Butterworth, 1971.

4 J. Adams, 'Life in a Global Village', *Environment and Planning*, December, 1972.

5 M. Harloe, 'No More Slogging On' (a review of Colin Buchanan's *The*

State of Britain, Faber and Faber, 1972), *RIBA Journal*, January, 1973.

6 Quoted by P. Clarke,'Site Value Rating and the Recovery of Betterment,' *Land Values*, P. Hall (Ed.), Sweet and Maxwell, 1965.

7 J. Thomson, *Motorways in London*, Duckworth, 1970.

8 A. Samuels, 'Compensation for Acquisition, Blight and Worsenment', *Journal of Planning and Property Law*, June, 1970.

9 *ibid.*

3 A brief history of betterment and worsenment

The study of present land problems and the promotion of future policies designed to reconcile the enigma of community created values requires some form of historical perspective from which, it is hoped, lessons may be derived.

Early attempts before 1909

Certain isolated attempts to recoup betterment have been made over the centuries. As far back as 1188 a Saladin Tithe was applied by Henry II to rents in order to fund the Third Crusade. Similar taxes were later levied by the Crown when appropriate consent had been registered with the Curia Regis and include an Act of 1427 which appointed Commissioners to collect a levy from those benefiting from land drainage and the construction of sea walls, and a similar Act of 1662 which sought to recover a portion of what was then described as 'melioration' regarding the increase in property values as a result of London street-widening schemes.

With the increasing expropriation of private land for public use throughout the nineteenth century, particularly for road, rail and canal construction, a standard code for assessing compensation upon compulsory purchase was devised, the Land Clauses Consolidation Act of 1845. This provided for additional payments, over and above open market value, to be made to owners for worsenment as a result of a 'forced sale'.

A growing realization that public undertakings enhanced the value of private property led to a rash of legislation around the turn of the century. Parker[1] describes the unsuccessful Strand Improvement Bill of 1890, the Cromwell Road Bridge Bill of 1892 and the more comprehensive London Improvement Bill of 1893 which collectively paved the way for the first enactment of its kind to reach the statute book, the Tower Bridge Southern Approach Act of 1895, which, like nine other London County Council Improvement Acts introduced between 1895 and 1902, permitted the authority to make a levy on the annual increase in the value of properties immediately benefiting from their road improvement schemes. The yields from such levies were disappointing, but, nevertheless, the principle was established.

1909 to 1939

Following a succession of attempts between 1902 and 1909 to introduce some form of site taxation, the Housing, Town Planning, Etc. Act 1909 authorized local authorities to prepare housing layout schemes on potential development land, and in recognition of the inevitable redistribution of values that would occur attempted to redress the balance by providing a general right for landowners to claim compensation for certain resultant losses and at the same time empowering the council concerned to levy a 50 per cent betterment charge. Despite problems of valuation and the natural reluctance of local authorities to incur compensation liabilities, the 1909 Act at least inaugurated the notion that some form of urban management and control was required and that such planning measures, whether permissive or restrictive, inevitably redistribute land and property values within the community, although in the first four years only two schemes were mounted.

A more sophisticated scheme, based upon the tenets of site value taxation, was introduced through the 'People's Budget' of 1909 and enshrined in the Finance Act 1910 whereby four kinds of tax were applied to land. Firstly, an *increment value duty* of 20 per cent chargeable on the increase in value of land upon disposition. Secondly, an *undeveloped land duty* levied at the rate of $\frac{1}{2}$d. in the £ every year on the site value of undeveloped land. Thirdly, a *reversion duty* taxable at 10 per cent and payable by a lessor on the value of his reversion at the end of the lease. Finally, a *mineral rights duty* imposed at 5 per cent per annum on mineral working rights. Problems of valuation and administration again led to a poor yield and eventual discontinuance before 1920. The Acquisition of Land (Assessment of Compensation) Act 1919 laid down the basic rules by which compensation is still largely assessed, and in doing so moved away from the principle of bonus payments for a 'forced sale' and towards open market value. After the 1919 Housing and Town Planning Act made it compulsory for councils to prepare development plans, and relatively minor changes were made in 1925, the next significant piece of legislation was the Town and Country Planning Act 1932 which increased the betterment levy from 50 to 75 per cent, extended the period of claim during which betterment might arise from three to twelve months, enlarged the owner's right to defer betterment payments but also restricted the rights to compensation in line with improving planning standards. It is a general measure of the caution displayed by authorities and a reflection of the ineffectiveness of the respective enactments between 1909 and 1939 that in order to avoid onerous compensation payments it has been estimated that despite only 143 planning schemes having been formally approved enough land was designated for development to accommodate approximately 290 million people against an actual population of around 40 million, and in respect of the betterment provisions only three occasions of charge were recorded.[2]

The Uthwatt Report

Following the Barlow and Scott Committee Reports on industry and agriculture respectively, an Expert Committee on Compensation and Betterment produced at a most critical period of the Second World War what has become known as the Uthwatt Report in 1942. In what still remains the most authoritative work on the subject the Committee made a number of recommendations. Firstly, that the development rights in undeveloped land should be vested in the state. All future land required for development would be compulsorily purchased at a value reflecting its existing use, and leased back at full open market value, thus recouping betterment. Secondly, if the land was 'dead-ripe' for development, plans having been prepared for it, it should still be acquired by the state but compensation would be full development value. Thirdly, developed land would only be acquired as and when necessary for planning schemes. The level of compensation would be assessed at full open market value as at 31 March 1939, thus, it was hoped, discouraging excess speculation. Fourthly, a levy, for example 75 per cent, would be imposed upon all increases in the value of land as from a particular date, with five-year revaluations. Fifthly, central government grants should be made available to local authorities to assist in the redevelopment of central areas.

In making their recommendations the committee had taken account of several problems that surround the issue of betterment-worsenment. Firstly, defining the amount of the increase in the value of land that was attributable to direct public policy, and not market forces, was problematical. Secondly, the valuation of respective interests was difficult. Thirdly, if compensation was to be paid for restriction development might 'shift' elsewhere, and so one authority might collect betterment whilst another was forced to pay worsenment. Fourthly, if compensation was to be made in full for restriction in development, the actual worsenment might 'float' over many properties and owners' claims would exceed actual damage. For these reasons the recommendations have a pragmatic rather than philosophical approach to the problem.[3]

The 1947 Act

The Uthwatt Report was only partially implemented by the Town and Country Planning Act 1947 which very briefly made planning subject to central control; vested *all* development rights in the state; made planning permission for all development obligatory; introduced a 100 per cent charge on the realized difference between development value and existing use value; established existing use value as the basis of compensation for compulsory purchase; and set up a Global Fund of £300 million to compensate those persons who lost existing development value.

For a number of reasons, including the shortage of materials, and the general restriction of development, as well as the 100 per cent Development Charge, the land market was stultified following the 1947 Act. A return to Conservative government resulted in the Town and Country Planning Acts of 1953 and 1954 which abolished the Development Charge, extinguished the Global Fund, converting the claims for loss of development rights into Unexpended Balances of Established Development Value, but anomalously still restricted the compensation for compulsory purchase to existing use value only. This anachronistic and manifestly unjust state of affairs whereby a dual level of values existed side by side was rectified by the 1959 Town and Country Planning Act which re-established an open market value for land compulsorily acquired. This Act was subsequently consolidated in the 1961 Land Compensation Act which still prevails.

The Land Commission Act

The next major enactment was the Land Commission Act 1967 which set up another central authority required to collect a Betterment Levy set initially at 40 per cent of development value, and with powers to purchase land net of levy, assemble land banks for prospective development, make Crownhold dispositions to facilitate desired development particularly in crisis areas, and generally acquire, manage and dispose of land in the interests of the community. It did not survive the change of government in 1970, being said to have neither stabilized prices nor facilitated the release of development land. Despite these criticisms it was really the stigma of betterment collection combined with the naive optimism of political punditry placing too great a premium upon the performance in early years which caused its dissolution. The full potential it possessed under the acquisition, management and disposal powers conferred by Part II of the Act whereby, acting as a land dealing agency, it would apply pressure upon recalcitrant planning authorities in the release of land, assisting and subsidizing central area residential redevelopment, agglomerating multi-various ownerships, aiding the process of reclamation, overriding parochial boundaries, and even facilitating private sector development by way of the 'middleman method', was never realized. It should, however, be recorded that whereas the proceeds of the levy were expected to amount to £80 million in a full year, 1968–9 raised £15 million and 1969–70 £31 million.

While it was intended that the Land Commission would have widespread powers to compulsorily purchase land, and do so on a basis which would leave the owner with the current use value plus a large slice of the development value as an incentive, it was recognized that it would be administratively impracticable for the Commission to buy all land required for development. Nevertheless, this power of acquisition, which could not be exercised until there was a positive planning decision attached to the land in question, was designed to be one of the most important features of the Act and was intended to combat what was thought to be the withholding of land with planning permission from the market by landowners. In such circumstances the Commission would step in, acquire the land and sell it on to builders and developers. The author undertook an extensive survey at the time in an attempt to identify if withholding of the kind described did, in fact, exist. It was discovered that very few landowners held land off the market, and those who did tended to have very small holdings and were not usually in the property industry as such. The problem appeared to be a very real shortage in land with planning permission despite the protestations of local planning authorities.

Between the abolition of the Land Commission and the introduction of Community Land legislation, which is dealt with more fully in Chapter 5, there occurred a series of *ad hoc* measures. A Department of the Environment circular 10/70, for example, exhorted local authorities to maintain the release of building land well in advance of demand and extra loan sanctions were proposed to enable local authorities to assemble such land banks. Additionally a land hoarding tax was suggested but never implemented. In December 1973 a tax on developers' profits was proposed by the then Conservative government and was enacted in Labour's 1974 Finance Act and reinforced existing Capital Gains Tax arrangements as applied to land. This Development Gains Tax is levied at prevailing corporation and income tax rates as appropriate but will be superseded by Development Land Tax charged at $66\frac{2}{3}$ per cent on the first £150 000 and 80 per cent on subsequent development value some time in 1976.

References

1 H. Parker, 'The History of Compensation and Betterment Since 1900', *Land Values*, P. Hall (Ed.), Sweet and Maxwell, 1965.
2 *ibid.*
3 J. Ratcliffe, *An Introduction to Town Planning*, Hutchinson, 1974.

4 Alternative solutions to the betterment and worsenment problem

In appraising the process of urbanization over the last hundred years, there appears to have been a persistent land problem. This problem centres around the formation of value and the incidence of blight consequent upon public action. As Hall[1] concisely states: 'Successive attempts have been made in legislation to find an answer to the problem of betterment. . . . The most important of these attempts have generated bitter party political controversy and have not survived later changes in government.' A felicitous statement in the light of the disaffection besetting the late Land Commission and the contentious provisions of current Community Land legislation. From past endeavours, it can be ascertained that any viable long-term solution must be not only technically feasible but also politically acceptable and administratively sound. In fact, a number of criteria upon which an acceptable solution to the betterment-worsenment dichotomy can be judged are discernible. The following list is compiled to assist clarity, being neither exhaustive nor definitive but merely a guide. Any satisfactory solution should be:

1 Permanent.
2 Acceptable.
3 A constant and continuing stimulus to investment and development in land. Not conducive to a stultification of the property market.
4 Administratively simple, understandable, enforceable, and not requiring the impossible of valuers.[2]
5 Designed to avoid arbitrariness, inaccuracy or inequity.[3]
6 Formulated so as to conform with the primary fiscal canons of feasibility, that is, economic neutrality and distributional equity.[4]
7 Drawn up to facilitate planning machinery.
8 Intended to promote comprehensive development and redevelopment.

9 Conceived so as to enhance good public and private estate management.

10 Generally prepared to ensure a more effective control of land.

Through time, a number of possible solutions have been suggested representing a spectrum of political thought and a continuum of practicability. These various solutions have broadly taken two different approaches to the problem. Some have attempted to provide what can be best described as a *once-and-for-all-time* solution. These include the recommendations of the Uthwatt Committee, the 1947 Town and Country Planning Act and more recently, albeit on an incremental basis, the Community Land legislation. They are founded upon the principle that virtually all increases in land value are attributable to the actions and growth of society and have therefore designed a single enactment to ensure that all subsequent development values accrue to the state with some allowance being made for compensation to mitigate transitional hardship. Others such as the 1909 Act and the 1974 Development Gains Tax have sought to secure a *continuing* solution which aims to reconcile the problems of betterment and worsenment as and when they arise. In this way development gains are taxed upon realization and development losses compensated upon incidence.

The nature of certain individual schemes aimed at reconciling the seemingly endless conflict have already been introduced, but in order to present as complete a picture as possible, the various proposals have been conveniently, albeit arbitrarily, grouped into those deemed to be radical reform, those of a more moderate character, and those advocating strictly limited measures. These chosen categories have no intrinsic significance.

Proposals for radical reform

In essence, the major programmes for radical reform embrace those schemes which aim at achieving a *total nationalization of all land* and two main problems surrounding the introduction of land nationalization as an immediate solution to the betterment-worsenment dilemma emerge.

The first is profoundly political. Any mention of the very term 'nationalization' is guaranteed to evoke a host of violent reactions, more usually with an emotional rather than rational content. The question of permanence is of paramount importance because 'any policy of nationalization that is to succeed must endure after today's government until and beyond tomorrow's'.[5]

The failure of the Development Charge and the brief life of the Betterment Levy ideally illustrate the notion that landowners and developers tend to discount the values implicit upon a potential future change of government. It could be argued that neither the 1947 nor the 1967 Acts approached total nationalization, and if a comprehensive scheme could be so devised that the complex nature of its provisions relating to tenure, taxation and domain defied expedient and inexpensive unravelling, radical reform might provide a more permanent solution.

The second major difficulty in respect of total nationalization is financial. If it were thought appropriate that the government should purchase all interests in land throughout Great Britain, the total sum involved would be of such proportions as to make the £300 million Global Fund of 1947 pale into insignificance. The operation would not necessarily involve direct or immediate funding out of taxation revenue, along with all the inherent inflationary repercussions, however, for it could be supported by way of a bond issue with the resultant interest charges being more than offset by the inevitable rental income, of whatever kind, that would accompany the implementation of such a scheme.

The financial problems, nevertheless, must not be minimized. The estimation of existing total land values is in itself a problematic exercise. Several calculations have been attempted such as those by Morris (1962)[6] who valued all British real estate at £20 500 million, Marber (1964)[7] who gauged it to be £150 000 million, and Clark (1965)[8] who estimated that land values alone amounted to £64 500 million. The relative consistency at that time of the latter two figures suggest that a realistic current figure might be in the region of £500 000 million. The administrative corollary to total and instantaneous nationalization is comprehensive and simultaneous valuation of all land and property in the country. An horrendous task.

Particular variations upon the general theme of nationalization have been propounded, the most notable of which is that entailing the *unification of the reversion*, whereby all land in the British Isles is nationalized but on an incremental basis over a long number of years. Such a scheme was considered, but not formally proposed, by the Uthwatt Committee,[9] which suggested:

That all land in Great Britain be forthwith converted into leasehold interests held by the present proprietors as lessees of the state at a pepper-corn rent for such uniform term of years as may be reasonably, without payment of compensation, be regarded as equitable, and subject to such conditions enforceable by re-entry as may from time to time be applicable under planning schemes.

The principal characteristic of this proposal is that it effectively avoids the payment of substantial sums in compensation. The only debatable matter is the length of the transitional term of years which is unlikely to be long enough to transcend the vagaries of political change.

A roughly similar scheme put forward in 1961 advocated that, on a chosen date, the freehold interest of all land would vest in the state without benefit of compensation, but with freeholders retaining a tenancy whose duration might be anything from nought to eighty years, depending upon the physical condition or 'life' of the building. Undeveloped land would receive an eighty-year lease and an eighty-year building lease upon development. During the statutory 'life' of the building the state would levy an increased rental to reflect any general increase in value and would arrange new leases for changes in use or redevelopment at rents which would take account of the altered circumstances. Compulsory acquisition would be at the existing use value of the statutory leasehold interest, and compensation for loss of development value would be limited. At the end of its statutory life, a building would become the property of the state and compensation would then be paid for the loss of the freehold on the basis of the existing use value of the site as on the vesting date augmented by a proportion, say 50 per cent, of any increase in value since that date.[10]

These contrived and rather extraordinary proposals entail not only enormous difficulties in terms of valuation practice but also present unnecessary problems in attaching inevitably arbitrary and spurious physical lives to buildings. Such a policy would, in all probability, prove politically extremely contentious. Moreover, compensation is paid for land values long after public acquisition, contradicting the underlying philosophy of betterment collection.

In general terms, the whole concept of land nationalization can be questioned. The need for absolute ownership and the flow of ensuing benefits has yet to be established. Present powers and controls have not been proved deficient, their exercise might merely be dilatory. Nationalization is likely to be politically unacceptable and thus impermanent. Furthermore, it could produce unforeseen and unfavourable economic consequences. On balance, state expropriation of all interests in land and property, whether on a once-and-for-all-time or on a continuing incremental basis, appears to create more problems than it solves.

Moderate reforms

A number of appealing and infinitely more pragmatic proposals to combat the betterment-worsenment problem have been promulgated which stop short of a complete transformation of the whole system of land ownership subsisting in Great Britain. Even land nationalization need not be permanent but could simply represent a temporary transfer for the reallocation of individual ownership. Temporary nationalization can be said to achieve a satisfactory unification of ownership to facilitate positive and comprehensive planning without necessarily debilitating the efforts of private development agencies. It would give local planning authorities greater flexibility in negotiating with both public and private sector landowners by means of 'trade-offs' in land, not only in different locations but also at different points in time. Such trading, however, could give rise to planning uncertainty and distributional inequity. Moreover, a compensation code which ignored the problems of shifting values would have to be devised. It would also be necessary to exact a betterment tax in order to collect unearned increments of development value, adequately compensate worsenment and make sufficient contributions to infrastructure costs. The main drawbacks would appear to be that the future continuing increments of betterment would be ignored on land subject to such transitory nationalization arrangements and, in the absence of alternative fiscal policies, the general betterment accruing to other land would escape entirely. Nevertheless, this system is successfully operated in West Germany on a selected local basis to facilitate urban renewal. If adopted, however, such a solution denotes a sledge-hammer and nut syndrome for it is surely more propitious to employ the existing precise and selective machinery of compulsory purchase to achieve the same ends.

More realistic moderate reforms that present themselves are the unification of development rights, management with advance public acquisition, site leasehold tenure, betterment levy, and site value rating.

Following in the footsteps of the 1947 Town and Country Planning Act, there are still those who favour a *unification of development rights*, whereby all development value is vested in the state whilst existing use value remains in the hands of the individual owner, thus virtually amounting to a 100 per cent betterment levy. This proposal permits planning agencies to apportion land irrespective of prevailing tenures and ensuing values, but, almost as a direct corollary, would forgo the financial correctives of the market unless the levy were pitched at a more acceptable rate, say 60 per cent. Although betterment is collected, moreover, the occasions are limited and there are no inherent provisions for worsenment.

Another 'moderate' solution involves the setting up of an agency responsible for ensuring the public ownership of land that is to be developed or redeveloped – a *Land Commission*. Such an agency was recommended in the Uthwatt Report and is not entirely dissimilar to the functions performed by New Town Development Corporations. The 1967 Land Commission was really only a partial affair, for in essence a fully effective Commission would be empowered to exercise rights of purchase in respect of land over a certain size for which planning permission was being sought. Such land would be subsequently leased back in a manner closely akin to the partnership schemes established between public authorities and private development agencies in central area development schemes over the years except that the promotion would be privately rather than publicly inspired. The main problems inherent in setting up and operating a Land Commission are almost certainly the scepticism of the market, the availability of funds, and the administrative complexity. The selective and partial nature of a Commission or National Development Agency, acting in isolation, implies that full collection of betterment is severely restricted unless accompanied by a comprehensive levy on development value, as was in fact the case in 1967. The proposal also fails to make significant provision for worsenment except by the purchase of blighted land at reparative values. Experience would suggest that a Commission as described would work best operating simply as a land agency unhampered by betterment collection which could then be left to the ordinary taxation system.

National estate management policies aimed at securing effective planning through public ownership have, in fact, a long tradition in many European countries. A large proportion of *advance municipal land acquisition* has been directed at the residential sector of the market, to such an extent that during the 1920s the governments of Denmark, Norway, Sweden, Finland, Holland, Germany, Austria,

Poland, Czechoslovakia, Switzerland, Italy, France and Spain, as well as Great Britain, all purchased land for public housing programmes in anticipation of real demand. Scandinavian countries in particular pursue a policy of encouraging and assisting local authorities to acquire land reserves. In Sweden, for example, where expropriation measures are admittedly slow and expensive the government has stated that: 'The municipalities should acquire land to such an extent that they would have a dominating influence on the supply of land likely to be used for community development within the foreseeable future.'[11]

The efficacy of this ambition is underlined by the domain of the City Council of Stockholm which owns three-quarters of the land that constitutes its area. In order to facilitate the acquisition of land, especially that for housing, government loans are available to municipalities and, although co-operative development schemes and those of private enterprise are encouraged, a system of site leases is favoured. Similarly in Norway, with increasing urbanization, there has been a marked tendency towards advance acquisition by local authorities. An interesting, and apparently unique method of acquiring land on the open market by mutual agreement is practised in Norway. Municipalities are given state bonds, with average maturities of about ten years, and where a landlord is induced by the local authority to sell his land, he is paid in bonds which, provided that he holds them until maturity, are exempt from any tax. Despite exemption from taxation and dividend accumulation at 'normal' rates of interest, it is unlikely that such a scheme would have been particularly attractive in this country with the immense capital growth encountered in property holding over the last few years.

Notwithstanding continental procedures, the practice and experience of public acquisition of land has evolved to a far greater degree in Great Britain. The obstacles to its further and more fruitful application in obtaining satisfactory development and redevelopment whilst at the same time recovering substantial sums of community created value, are, firstly, the illogical basis, apart from New Towns and Action Areas, upon which compensation for compulsory purchase is assessed; secondly, the short-sighted and parsimonious attitude on the part of central government in not making available adequate funds or appropriate powers for public commercial development; and, thirdly, the prevalent traditional approach towards the proprietary holding of land and the individual procurement of development value.

The creation of a climate favouring a more adventurous programme of public land acquisition does not automatically imply absolute or perpetual control of tenure. Through the intelligent introduction of *leasehold tenure* a number of desirable objectives could be attained. Significantly, the manifest advantages implicit in establishing a system of site leaseholds was recognized by the Uthwatt Committee (1942) and included in the Development Rights Scheme. This was subsequently ignored, although it would probably have provided a most efficient form of managing urban development, as well as helping to solve the problem of betterment collection. As Archer[12] explains: 'The two essential features of the site leasehold system of urban development are the unification of the landowner, planning and land development functions, and the continuation of the landowner interest by limiting the land interest of building owners to a site lease.'

Leasehold tenure as a mode of land management has a long and chequered history,[13] but a number of advantages can be easily distinguished. Through site rentals, a substantial proportion of betterment value can be collected on an annual basis and adjusted at appropriate intervals. Whilst levying a charge on the unearned increment it still permits sufficient financial return to stimulate the private sector of development. It allows and encourages the continued functioning of the property market, which, with its demand-orientated perspective, provides a medium for a recognition of consumer preference. The ultimate or eventual power for reorganization of individual leasehold interests and their redistribution on a more efficient basis is retained. In the same way, comprehensive redevelopment through reassembly when appropriate is facilitated, as is the proper and corporate provision of services, amenities and facilities of all kinds. Moreover, site preparation and construction works can be undertaken at an economic scale and general estate management contracts can be placed and supervised on a comprehensive and continuative basis. By automatically internalizing a wider range of cost and benefits than is usual in private estate development, municipal site leasehold tenure provides a common interest uniting tenants, thus stimulating community action, citizen participation and corporate responsibility. The detailed day-to-day trivia of planning control can be incorporated into leasehold covenants enhancing individual certainty while preserving public amenity. The public landowners' long-term view precludes short-run exploitation, in addition to which the speculation occasioned by dilatory development can be prevented by including terms in the lease requiring prompt con-struction. Finally, the allocation of sites on leasehold tenancies based upon periodic rent reviews permits a flexible management policy towards land values, not only in the recovery of betterment but also in mitigating the incidence of worsenment and in the promotion or discouragement of particular forms of development.

Against this array of inherent advantages contained in a system of municipal site leaseholds must be set the cost of initial implementa-tion, the vulnerability to political interference, the multitude of statutory restrictions, the present inadequate and incompatible means of financing house purchase, the propagation by all major British political parties of freehold home ownership, and the sus-picion from the commercial sector of public encroachment upon tenure.

The introduction of any scheme advocating a system of national land management is frequently accompanied by proposals for the imposition of a *betterment levy* aimed at collecting a proportion of unearned increment either at discrete intervals, or on specific occasions such as the granting of a lease or the conveyance of a freehold. Several variations have been advanced over the last eighty years and a number tried. The most notable of these attempts have already been described. The main criticism levelled at any form of betterment charge is the deleterious effect on the land and property market, particularly if the charge is levied at 100 per cent. The aim should therefore be to design a scheme which collects a high propor-tion of betterment as well as safeguarding the continued functioning of the land market. To achieve this landowners should be left that portion of development value, but only just that portion, which is sufficient to persuade them to bring their land on to the market, the residue being collected as betterment. As the potential profit to the landowner rises, that is the greater is the difference between existing use value and value in an alternative use, so the proportion of this difference or development value which is collected in levy should rise correspondingly. It has been tentatively suggested[14] that if the new value is twice that of the old, the rate of levy should be 60 per cent, if thrice it should be 70 per cent, and in the event of the new value being several times that of the old, the levy could be pitched as high as 90 per cent, still leaving the landowner with what can be described as 'sweetener'.

The fundamental deficiency of most betterment levy solutions is that they neglect the payment of worsenment. One method which is said to take this into account is *site value rating*. The underlying principles of land value taxation have already been discussed[15] and a detailed examination of its operation is beyond the restricted scope of this text. But in the context of providing an answer to the betterment-worsenment problem it would seem that to recoup all betterment, the tax would have to be levied at a rate equivalent to the annual value of the whole of the increase in value occasioned by improved circumstances. As this rate would apply to the whole of the existing use value as well, however, it has been suggested that the market value of land would theoretically be reduced to zero![16] Moreover, site value rating does not provide the most satisfactory vehicle for the payment of worsenment as is commonly supposed, for to be practicable it would be necessary to settle for a rate well below 100 per cent which would not provide for an equitable level of compensation. In many ways, the net result of site value rating is almost identical to that which can be achieved by a system of state leaseholds under one or other of the nationalization proposals, its only possible merit being that of political acceptability.

Limited reform

As with any other legal code, the legislation relating to land and land values, together with their respective private privileges and public powers, is constantly undergoing revision. The increasing impact of large-scale urban development and the growing awareness of the intrusive consequences to community rights and personal property values has focussed attention on the more serious anomalies and omissions pertaining to our present laws concerning the payment of compensation for worsenment and the collection of betterment. A succession of reports prepared by a variety of bodies have been presented during the last few years. Their recommendations are referred to as limited because they all seek to remedy the existing and disparate defects in the current compensation code. The limited and partial nature of their proposals highlights the inadequacy of our present approach to the problem. Nevertheless, though partial and piecemeal in their provisions, their promotion and application deserves review in this study because of the political impracticability and crushing administrative burden underlying radical, permanent and comprehensive changes in land tenure, taxation and proprietary interest. Even where the social system or prevailing school of political philosophy favours a total transference of land ownership and redistribution of development value, limited reform retains an important role either in any transitory arrangements preceding final implementation of radical policy, or as a precursory medium-term solution pending a more opportune climate.

Several significant partial proposals have been advanced over the last decade culminating in the Land Compensation Act 1973 and the Development Gains Tax 1974. In 1966, for example, the Greater London Council, concerned about the financial repercussions of their urban motorway programme upon private property values, and the anomalously unjust situation caused by the rules contained in *McCarthy* v. *Metropolitan Board of Works* (1884) relating to compensation for injurious affection when no land is taken, sought to mitigate the hardship in three ways. Firstly, they suggested that they should be allowed to acquire by agreement property outside the statutory line of a highway but so obviously affected, and to such an extent, that it could not be disregarded. Secondly, they should be permitted to carry out or to make grants to landowners towards the cost of carrying out remedial works such as sound-proofing. Thirdly, in order to secure integrated planning schemes, they wished to be allowed to compulsorily acquire property for environmental purposes. It is worth noting that in forwarding these proposals Blessley[17] expresses considerable doubt as to the feasibility of public participation in view of the blight directly resulting from the publication of a range of possible alternative proposals. He illustrates his argument by reference to the now hypothetical case of the London Ringway 2 section between Norbury and Falconwood where the Greater London Council team examined twenty-nine alternative alignments. Clearly, if all had been published, blight would have been very extensive indeed.

Following the GLC proposals, a joint committee of the Chartered Land Societies (1968) published a report containing the following proposals for limited reform:

1 The rules governing compensation for injurious affection when no land is taken should be assimilated to those which apply when land is taken. A compulsory purchase order might define lands not taken to which the rules could apply.
2 A claim for injurious affection might be delayed up to two years to determine the impact of the new user.
3 Compensation for disturbance should cover all consequential loss subject to a reasonable test of remoteness. Loss suffered prior

to the notice to treat should be included if it is a result of the scheme in question.

4 A displaced residential owner-occupier forced to purchase a more expensive house should be granted an interest-free loan secured on that house.

5 The qualifying categories for blight set out in Section 138 of the 1962 Town and Country Planning Act (now Section 192 of the 1971 Act) should be widened. The power to serve a blight notice should apply when only part of a hereditament has been blighted.

6 Compensation for disturbance should be payable to those who have been obliged to serve a blight notice.

At about the same time, a committee of 'Justice' in 1969 made certain similar recommendations relating to the general field of compensation upon compulsory acquisition and the remedies for planning restrictions. Both reports exemplified the accent that has been repeatedly placed upon paying compensation for certain types of worsenment and the constant neglect, prior to the Community Land legislation, of establishing a system which not only takes into account the full depreciating ramifications of planning proposals but also sets out to recoup the enhanced values. This situation is perpetuated in the Land Compensation Act 1973, which, in attempting to legislate for the impact of major public projects on their immediate environment, has adopted a number of the foregoing proposals not already incorporated within various enactments relating to planning and compensation. Its main provisions are as follows:

1 For the first time the Act spells out a right of compensation to certain landowners when property is depreciated by the use of new public works although no part of the land is taken.

2 The period during which compensation can be claimed is extended so that the full impact of the scheme can be taken into account.

3 The proposal put forward by the GLC recently reiterated by the Urban Motorways Committee, regarding the mitigation of noise pollution by imposing a duty upon public authorities to undertake insulation and other works where appropriate, is given statutory effect.

4 Wider powers of acquisition designed to ameliorate any adverse effects of public works are granted.

5 Under Part III a compendium of provisions extending the remuneration for people displaced from land is introduced.

6 The 'nonsense' practised in the past whereby compensation for injurious affection was assessed according to the use to which the claimant's land was to be put and not the whole of the works is removed.

7 Statutory effect is given to the making of advances of compensation payments.

8 The practice of reducing compensation upon compulsory acquisition on account of the fact that the acquiring authority are providing alternative accommodation is forbidden.

9 The Act attempts to allow for the service of blight notices at an earlier stage in the planning process. An awkward provision to implement given the uncertainty of strategic planning.

Despite undeniable merits these reforms merely plug existing loopholes in compensation law. Nothing is included to collect betterment. The only three ways in which this is currently pursued are the anachronistic provisions of Section 7 of the Land Compensation Act 1961 relating to 'set-off', admirable in themselves but inappropriate in isolation, the imposition of a development gains tax, and the comparatively rare occurrences when planning agencies are able to employ a system of recoupment whereby land over and above immediate requirements for particular public uses is acquired and the ensuing gains which fall on that land as a result of public works are automatically captured.

European comparisons

Despite membership of the European Economic Community information regarding comparative land management systems is extremely difficult to obtain. Nevertheless, a brief description of varying approaches and policies provides a useful and interesting context within which to judge our own.

Sweden, for example, has an extremely long history of planning dating from the setting up in 1635 of a city planning office in Stockholm to co-ordinate redevelopment occasioned by the frequent fires resulting from largely wood structures. Early leasehold occupation from the Crown slowly gave way to increasing freehold tenure until in 1866 a comprehensive redevelopment plan for Stockholm was frustrated by the costly levels of compensation. To reverse this trend in 1904 the city purchased 2000 hectares of surrounding development land at a time when the developed area was only 1700 hectares, and three years later legislation was introduced which permitted municipalities to dispose of land only on a leasehold basis in order to maintain planning control and discourage speculation. This process continued until, by the outbreak of the Second World War, almost all the remaining undeveloped land, some 12 600 hectares, had been acquired. A further power was conferred upon municipalities in 1953 by which they were empowered to acquire land in advance of a statutory plan, a radical step, shared only with France in Western Europe. Although during the 1960s attention was turned to the acquisition of developed land in areas of urban renewal, problems of capital, particularly outside Stockholm, were encountered and government aid was introduced in 1966 to supplement the lack of private funds. The following year, in pursuit of an active land policy, Sweden decided that local authorities should control all future development land and in 1968 pre-emption rights were introduced, whereby an authority has first refusal on all sales of land, compensation being assessed on open market value. Additionally, local authorities are required to purchase land up to twenty years in advance of need and, despite slow and cumbersome acquisition procedures, advance land acquisition policies appear to have facilitated the planning mechanism and stabilized land values.

Another country with a relatively long planning history is *Holland*, and parallels can be drawn with Sweden. Ever since 1896, for example, Amsterdam has pursued a policy of leasing land and now all local authorities tend to acquire development land with compensation being assessed on an existing use value basis. Management schemes vary, however, for whereas Amsterdam lets its land at 4 per cent of cost per annum for co-operative housing and 6 per cent for other uses, Rotterdam sells housing land at cost, sells commercial land at full market value and leases industrial land at rack rentals. In this way land for housing is considered a public service and is always provided at cost and it is interesting to note that 41 per cent of new housing is provided by co-operatives. The very extensive advance land acquisition policy has effectively checked the extreme inflation in land values so prevalent in other European countries, particularly in respect of agricultural land surrounding cities.

Land-use planning in *France* is typically centralized and of comparatively recent origin. Again, in an effort to counteract inflation wide powers of expropriation are available, both to central government, including the regional prefectures, and to local authorities. These powers may be exercised to assemble land banks even if no approved development plan exists for the area and compensation is based upon existing use value. In 1958 Zones for Priority Development were introduced as a further measure against land value speculation whereby within a designated Zone prices are frozen, pre-emption upon sale is available to local authorities, development is directed towards the Zone and land uses are very strictly controlled. Speculation nevertheless continued and in 1962 a further enactment provided for Zones for Deferred Planning where development was not immediately expected and where pre-emption was restricted to eight years from designation and planning powers less onerous. By 1970, 237 000 hectares lay in Deferred Planning Zones which provide for an eight-year national land bank. In addition, France possesses a complicated array of land and property taxes including an annual rate of 0·5 per cent, a betterment tax of 60 per cent on a generously calculated development value, a building tax, a planning tax, an over-development levy, and an equalization tax which collects development value falling upon land outside public works but has benefited as a result of them.

Spain is another country subject to central control where comprehensive planning control dates from 1956 and again expropriation operated by Ministry-run Land Directorates is available, but only for housing and public building. Compensation is assessed according to a registered value based upon a four-yearly cadastral survey and which includes hope value. In line with France, great emphasis is placed upon taxation measures to effect planning policies. Among a number of other imposts are a 25 per cent development gains tax, a vacant site tax and perhaps most novel of all a power to compel private development in certain urban areas without appropriating land. There is also a central land agency, the Gerencia de Urbanización, whose responsibility it is to purchase land, provide infrastructure and put it on to the market for residential development at non-speculative prices often to joint enterprise companies held jointly by private builders and local authorities.

Land policy in *West Germany* is highly decentralized and left largely in the hands of the local authorities. Despite this, public acquisition of land has been fairly rapid, up to 50 per cent of some of the larger cities such as Munich being in public ownership. Compensation is based upon open market value although stringent betterment levy provisions are in the course of preparation for all those transactions which include an element of development value. Probably the most interesting German innovation is a method of temporary nationalization whereby in redevelopment schemes all land is unified within public ownership and re-allotted according to the development plan with both betterment and worsenment being accounted for. Land which passes through this form of public ownership is normally leased or sold with the condition that it should be developed, and while most development occurs in the private sector, default powers rest with the authority.

While notionally *Italy* has a centralized land policy and a planning system dating back to 1865, the Latin temperament of local authorities militates against conformity in implementation. Nevertheless, necessary land may be publicly acquired following an approved plan. A municipality will purchase all the land and then invite tenders from the previous owners. If none are forthcoming then the public may openly tender. An interesting alternative approach which transfers responsibility to the private sector is the use of pooling schemes whereby the owners of 75 per cent of an area affected by a plan may form an association expropriating the rest. It is worthy of note that such an device was in fact examined in the Uthwatt Report and might well find favour in this country again.

Most local authorities in *Denmark* pursue an active land policy but are severely hampered by very limited powers of compulsory purchase and advance acquisition is effected at open market levels. There are, however, very stringent capital gains taxes on land dealing which are underpinned by a four-yearly cadastral survey and the production of land value maps.

In *Norway* and *Finland* the profits on the sale of land are taxed as income with a resultant slowing-up of the land market. In Norway, land prices are subject to government control but in Finland, where municipal land holding in urban areas is very high, often between 50 and 70 per cent, there is an exemption from tax after land has been owned for ten years. Again, immobility and a reduction in supply often result.

The situation is obviously very different in Eastern Europe where land speculation is generally unacceptable and private investment is not usually sought for public works. The *USSR* unambiguously abolished the private ownership of land in 1917, but policies in other Communist countries vary. In *Poland*, for example, land ownership differs from city to city, for, whereas the whole of Warsaw is nationalized, as are a few other towns in the north, most urban land is privately owned and the proportion is increasing. Nevertheless, if land is not developed in accordance with an approved plan within six years it is liable to expropriation. *Hungary* also has private ownership but on a much more limited scale, and compulsory purchase powers are available to local authorities if land is not properly developed within two years with compensation assessed at fixed historic values. In *Romania, Yugoslavia,* and *East Germany,* similar systems exist with land ownership being divided into three basic categories – state, co-operative and personal.

References

1 P. Hall, *Land Values,* Sweet and Maxwell, 1965.
2 N. Lichfield, 'Land Nationalisation', *Land Values,* P. Hall (Ed.), Sweet and Maxwell, 1965.
3 U. Hicks, 'Can Land be Assessed?', *Assessment of Land Values,* D. Holland (Ed.), TRED, 1970.
4 D. Holland, *Assessment of Land Value,* TRED, 1970.
5 A. George, unpublished diploma thesis on compensation and betterment, Oxford Polytechnic, 1971.
6 V. Morris, unpublished M.Sc. thesis on compensation and betterment, University of London, 1962.
7 P. Marber, 'Nationalisation of Property', *Chartered Surveyor,* 1964.
8 C. Clark, 'Land Taxation: Lessons from International Experience', *Land Values,* P. Hall (Ed.), Sweet and Maxwell, 1965.
9 A. Uthwatt (Chairman), *Expert Committee on Compensation and Betterment,* Cmnd. 6386, HMSO, 1942.
10 Lichfield, *op. cit.*
11 Housing and Urban Development Department, *Urban Land Policy – Selected Aspects of European Experience,* HUD-94-SF, 1969.
12 R. Archer, *Urban Planning and the Property Market,* School of Environmental Studies, UCL, 1971.
13 I. McDonald, 'The Leasehold System', *Urban Studies,* vol. 6, June, 1969.
14 A. Day, 'The Case for Betterment Charges', *Land Values,* P. Hall (Ed.), Sweet and Maxwell, 1965.
15 See Chapter 1.
16 George, *op. cit.*
17 K. Blessley, 'Compensation and Blight in an Urban Environment', *Estates Gazette,* 6 March 1971.

5 Community Land legislation

The most recent attempt to resolve the vexatious question of community created land values and the related problems of planning and development is the Community Land Act 1975. Before making any critical assessment of these proposals it is necessary to set out the principal measures contained in the legislation.

The Community Land Act

The Community Land Act which gained Royal Assent in November 1975 is designed to implement the proposals contained in the White Paper on Land (Cmnd. 5730) dealing with the community ownership of development land and the acquisition of unoccupied office blocks. The White Paper set out the objectives of the government's land policy as:

(a) to enable the community to control the development of land in accordance with its needs and priorities; and
(b) to restore to the community the increase in value of land arising from its efforts.

The Act attempts to provide a framework for ensuring that ultimately the vast majority of all development takes place on land which is in, or has passed through, public ownership. It is thought that this will enable the community by its ownership of land to control positively the form and rate of development.

Public authorities will be empowered by the Community Land legislation to buy land at a price excluding development value. Eventually this will be brought about by changing the basis of compensation to current use value. For a transitional period, however, the basis of compensation will continue to be market value, but the actual cost of land to local authorities will be reduced by enabling them to buy at a price which excludes the amount of development land tax that would have been payable had the vendor sold privately. The detailed arrangements for this transitional period appear in the Development Land Tax Act.

In essence the Act provides for the essential powers and duties of local authorities leaving a number of important matters to be dealt with in subordinate legislation or by administrative means. There still exists, therefore, a high degree of uncertainty regarding the way in which the scheme is put into practice over time. The operation of the scheme will be in the hands of local authorities and new town corporations, except in Wales where a new Land Authority will be established to exercise the functions of the legislations. It is envisaged that considerable local variation will occur in respect of the way in which the scheme will operate according to local circumstances. Both county and district councils will be 'authorities' for the purpose of the Act. It is provided that they should have prepared agreements relating to the way in which their respective functions will be exercised in particular County Areas by the beginning of 1976. It will also be possible for authorities to form Joint Boards or Joint Committees to handle their land acquisition and management schemes. If local authorities fail to operate the scheme provision is made for the Secretary of State to transfer the responsibility to himself, to another authority, or to a specially constituted agency.

The objectives of the Act relate to *development land*. This is defined as land which is, in the opinion of the authority concerned, suitable for relevant development. In considering this question of suitability local authorities will still be required to act within the existing planning framework. The government hope, however, that the scheme will help to make the present system of planning more effective and to ensure that development is more positively planned with local authorities being required to look up to ten years ahead in planning their programmes of land acquisition. The scope of 'relevant development' will be defined in regulations made under the legislation but will certainly exclude what is considered to be minor development not significant for the purposes of the land scheme.

The responsible authorities will be given the new powers and duties outlined below as from the *first appointed day* and, as soon as local authorities are able to take on the task, 'relevant date' orders and 'commencement' orders will be made which apply the legislation. These orders conferring a duty to bring land into public ownership will be made progressively area by area and type of development by type of development. In this way categories of development which will have been designated as coming within what is described as 'the full duty' in any area will not occur except on land which is in, or has passed through, public ownership.

On a *second appointed day*, which will not be introduced until all local authorities are applying the transitional powers to the public ownership of land consequent upon development proposals, the basis of compensation will be changed to current use value as opposed to open market value subject to Development Land Taxation.

In this way there will in effect be three stages to the scheme. Stage 1 which occurs before a full duty is imposed upon authorities to ensure that land passes through public ownership but where authorities should still be considering the desirability of bringing development land into public ownership. Stage 2 where a full duty is imposed in a particular area to bring land into public ownership but compensation is still at open market value but the cost to local authorities is reduced by the deduction of Development Land Tax which could ultimately rise to 100 per cent. Stage 3 where a full duty is imposed upon all local authorities throughout the country and compensation for public acquisition prior to development is assessed at current use value.

Following the first appointed day, therefore, local authorities not only have a general duty to have regard to the desirability of bringing development land into public ownership but also have a duty either to develop such land themselves or to make it available for development by others. Because of the wider powers available to local authorities as a result of this legislation the government intend that these authorities should pay regard to a number of factors. These would include the provisions of the development plan, likely needs of the present and future local community, and the requirements of local industrial and commercial concerns, statutory undertakers, builders and developers.

As indicated above, it is foreseen that as local authorities build up their resources and expertise the Secretary of State will make orders applying a full duty publicly to acquire land upon more areas and upon more types of development. Although certain categories of development might be either temporarily or permanently exempted from the duties imposed by the Community Land Act this will not prevent local authorities from acquiring such land if it facilitates desirable development. Further advice regarding these circumstances is expected from the Department of the Environment in

C

due course. It is intended that the legislation should confer on local authorities new powers of land acquisition on a much wider basis. They will have the power to acquire both by agreement with private landowners and by way of compulsory purchase subject to confirmation by the Secretary of State. For the purpose of such acquisition a wide definition of 'relevant development' is envisaged.

It is currently proposed that certain modifications will be made under the new powers where compulsory purchase takes place. These are likely to include firstly, that compulsory purchase orders made under the new powers will not have to specify the precise purpose for which land is being acquired; secondly, the Secretary of State will have the power to disregard objections made on the grounds that the acquisition was unnecessary or inexpedient; and thirdly, the Secretary of State will no longer be required to hold an inquiry or hearing into objections but will, if necessary, be able to decide questions of compulsory purchase by way of written representations.

Although the legislation does not include any new procedures for designating development land it is proposed that in order to allow local authorities to safeguard their position in respect of public acquisition of development land they will be able to designate areas known as *disposal notification areas*. Within such an area anyone proposing to dispose of a substantial interest in land would first be required to inform the local authority, and they in turn would be able to say whether or not they proposed to acquire the relevant interest. Blight notice procedure under the 1971 Town and Country Planning Act would apply in circumstances where the local authority elected to acquire.

In addition to the areas which they themselves have identified for development within the framework of agreed planning policies, local authorities will be given an opportunity to seek to acquire land which is identified through the making of a planning application. In this context, where an authority are considering an application for planning permission in respect of relevant development they will be required to serve a notice stating whether or not they wish to acquire the land concerned. They will also be able to serve a notice stating their intention not to purchase subject to conditions such as an early start to development. Where an authority do serve a notice indicating their intention to purchase and subsequently planning permission is granted, that planning permission will be suspended pending the settlement of the public acquisition. The local authority would have a year in which to serve a compulsory purchase notice which would then be subject to the normal procedures. If they do not wish to acquire, or serve a conditional notice which is complied with, or in some other way fail to pursue the question of acquisition the suspension of planning permission is lifted and the local authority lose their power to acquire the land under the new compulsory purchase powers for five years.

It is intended that local authorities will be required to make proper arrangements for the management of land and that all disposals of land by them shall be subject to the consent of the Secretary of State. They will also be expected to dispose of land on the best terms that can reasonably be obtained. Although it is envisaged that all land for private residential development will be disposed of freehold by way of building agreements directly to the eventual occupier, land for other developments will normally be disposed of leasehold with rent review provisions built-in and the length of the lease restricted. Local authorities will be required to give prior consideration in granting the opportunity for undertaking development to the owner of the land or the applicant for planning permission.

It is proposed that the financing of the scheme will be on a capital basis and outside the normal arrangements for the financing of local authority activities. This will be done by way of borrowing and repayments will be made out of disposal receipts. Furthermore, borrowing for land acquisition will become a new key sector in terms of loan sanction based upon a five-year rolling expenditure programme submitted annually. Where local authorities' land accounts come into surplus that surplus will be distributed according to the following formula: 40 per cent will be payable to the Secretary of State for payment into the Consolidated Fund, 30 per cent will be available to the individual authority or authorities concerned and the remaining 30 per cent will be divided up between other local authorities by the Secretary of State. The method of assisting first-time house buyers is still being considered.

It is estimated that following the second appointed day public authorities will be receiving in total some £350 million a year as a result of the changed basis of compensation and a further £500 million will be yielded up as a result of land trading. It is further estimated that by that time an additional 12 000 staff will be required to implement the scheme. Approximately 4000 of these will have to be senior qualified staff.

An assessment

With a changing economic and political climate towards land there can now be very few people involved with planning and development who would deny the basic objectives of the Act in trying both to achieve more effective planning and to recoup some measure of community created value. What remains in very serious doubt is whether this most recent enactment is the most appropriate vehicle for implementing a policy of land reform. While undeniably standing as a statement of radical political philosophy it still reflects a fundamentally superficial analysis of the land problem.

Looking back at the suggested criteria for a satisfactory and continuing solution set out in the last chapter it seems that little has been learnt from the past. The lack of political consensus as to the scheme's acceptability is unlikely to produce permanence; there is no inherent investment incentive but a high degree of probability that the property market will dry up; it is administratively complex, will require considerable valuation skill and will produce both political and professional arbitrariness; the high level of accompanying development land tax hardly possesses economic neutrality; and the beneficial effects upon planning machinery are hard to divine.

Attendant criticism has emerged from a much wider spectrum of opinion than was probably expected. The major points of concern can be usefully summarized as follows:

1   Basic conflicts of interest are bound to emerge in a variety of circumstances. There will be conflicts of interest between central and local government devolving around political commitment, interpretation and implementation; between first-tier and second-tier authorities of varying political complexions and professional attitudes; similarly between competing second-tier authorities who may either be vieing for growth or contesting for conservation; finally, there will be a conflict within individual local authorities between the functions of community planning on the one hand and desired development on the other, a situation which is likely to place both officers and members alike in invidious and exposed positions.

2   Disturbing amendments are made to the existing compulsory purchase procedures. All rights to a hearing or a public inquiry are abolished; an acquiring authority is no longer obliged to state the

purpose for which the land is required; the Secretary of State is entitled to ignore completely objections that question either the necessity or expedience of the acquisition; he is also empowered to grant consent for the acquisition of land for purposes that would otherwise be *ultra vires.*

3   Far too many provisions relating to the operation of the scheme rely upon delegated legislation, there being an unprecedented array of discretionary powers. In the same vein, the authority conferred upon the Secretary of State is exceptionally far-reaching. He determines the kind of development land to which the Act applies; sets the various dates by which the programme of the Act is brought into force; decides which parts of the scheme shall apply to what parts of the country and when; controls the acquisition of development land through his powers to confirm or reject compulsory purchase orders; directs the use of land by requiring local authorities to seek his consent before any appropriation, development or disposition of land; is responsible for determining all the functions of local authorities in respect of the Act; and retains the right to transfer all or any of these functions to another authority without having to give a reason. It is not without justification that the Secretary of State has been described as 'a veritable dictator of development'.[1] In any event there would certainly appear to be a general dissipation of public accountability.

4   Grave doubts can be cast as to local authorities' ability regarding the 'identification of development land' which is naturally a fundamental prerequisite to the effective operation of the Act. The recent conflicting evidence as to land availability for residential development in the South East highlights the problem. On the one hand, a private report by Shankland Cox portrays a deficit of between 20 000 and 35 000 dwellings a year up to 1981 on a present rate of approximately 70 000 a year, whereas the Standing Conference on London and South East Regional Planning entirely refutes such predictions and protests sufficiency. The gulf between strategic planning and practical implementation is a very wide one. Identification of development land by private sector agencies under the new legislation also has certain anomalies, because absolutely anybody has the right to apply for planning permission on anybody else's land and having attracted the attention of the local authority, who then purchase it at current use value or net of development value, have a privileged position to buy the land back and develop it. The

possibilities under this provision have colourfully been described as 'creating a legion of bounty hunters bringing in land dead or alive for the local authorities'.[2]

5   Apart from the disparities that will arise as a result of differing approaches to the drawing up of land acquisition and management schemes by various local authorities, there is a distinct danger that such documents will become little more than a form of words, fulfilling statutory requirements but protecting individual authorities' vested interests. Perhaps the government are not aware that proverbial 'bloodbaths' have occurred in many parts of the country as a result of county and district 'dialogue'.

6   There would seem to be a dichotomy in government policy between the need to provide an extra £4000 million in the development field over the next two years, and the general constraint being exercised upon public expenditure. Furthermore, although the Secretary of State contends that there will be no charge on the rates it is unlikely that the consequent delays of local authority acquisition, the extra participatory procedures inherent in public sector planning and development, and the costs of development finance will ensure that rate revenues are protected in the early transitional stages.

7   The transitional period is also likely to witness the incidence of planning blight on a vast scale as recourse is made by local authorities to informal plans and land programmes.

References

1 D. Widdicombe, 'The Community Land Bill – A Commentary', *Estates Gazette*, 17 May 1975.
2 H. Rossi, 'Community Land – The Conservative Viewpoint', *Estates Gazette*, 21 June 1975.

6 Planning

Although the market mechanism continues to perform its traditional function of allocation within broad land-use categories, open market values increasingly become an expression of planning policy and statutory control. The expression is not always a reflection of the spirit and purpose of the original policy. All too often, the level and distribution of values indicate the inadequacy or misdirection of particular strategies. Furthermore, the speculative nature of subsisting values is a function of the poor performance of past policies and the uncertainty of future ones. The lack of rapport between the concurrent processes of planning and development, which in theory should be complementary but in practice commonly appear contradictory, tend to support George Bernard Shaw's cynical observation that 'All professions are conspiracies against the laity.' In this context, a considerable amount of controversy currently rages around the role and function of the planning profession. For example, should it be a technical value-free activity or a politically inspired agent of social change? Despite the accredited adoption of a systems approach towards decision-making in an urban and regional planning context, the continued polarization of argument between social planning on the one hand and physical land-use planning on the other, ignores the vital interrelationship between the two. This connection is epitomized by the social problems thrown up by the irregularities of land tenure and the anomalies caused by the disjointed and incremental control exercised by planning authorities over it. Even in accepting the most extreme arguments advocating the planners' role as an agent of social change, there still remains the need to comprehend and manipulate the functioning of the land market, preventing wasteful and self-destructive competition, but at the same time maintaining a condition of scarcity and certainty that secures the expectation of profits. This almost Keynesian approach towards physical land-use planning is increasingly vituperative to growing sections of the social sciences.

As Moor maintains,[1] the conventional approach of the planning profession to a free market in land is one of hostility. This attitude is illustrated by the underlying motives that all too often influence the direction of planning control, for the controls which have been erected not only attempt to limit the growth of the city as such, but also try to limit the power of the entrepreneur.

Despite this traditional hostility, the planner is compelled to act within a society generally amenable to market operations, where the initiative to develop land allocated in plans for future growth has lain largely with private enterprise. Consequently, in order to attain the social and environmental objectives that are set by the community, he is obliged to function as an agent of the market, synthesizing views, co-ordinating action and unifying interests. This responsibility is not restricted to the conventional practice of land assembly and provision of infrastructure facilities, but should extend to the function of prompting and facilitating the various agencies and forces of the development process in such a way that the speculative element which currently dominates the operation of the market is superseded. In this way, the added certainty supporting the investment decision should entice private sector involvement at remunerative levels more in line with the general equity market. If dividends from property investment could be stabilized in this way, so that they represent what are considered to be 'normal returns', then a substantial proportion of economic rent or betterment would be available for collection. The mistrustful relationship presently prevailing between the planning and development processes exercises a serious debilitating effect upon successful environmental management.

Positive planning

The government's White Paper on Land, which was the philosophical progenitor of recent Community Land legislation, places great emphasis upon the need for 'positive planning'. It does little, however, to demonstrate what exactly this is, or how it might be achieved, apart from proposing a system which ensures that development land passes through the hands of public ownership, apparently in blissful ignorance that planning as a function does not always concern itself with development or growth. Positive planning must in effect assume some form of operational activity which puts the theory of planning into practice. Employing the terminology of the planning profession, this describes the *implementation* stage of the planning process, and in a mixed economy the implementation of policy involves a wide and varied array of agencies, not merely the clearly identifiable public and private agencies at the extremes of the market, but also miscellaneous hybrid breeds of both. This being so, the form of relationship and degree of rapport between policy makers on the one hand and the agents of execution on the other is of prime concern in the effectuation of positive planning. Moreover, it is the land ownership involvement of implementation agencies, and the ensuing financial repercussions of their activities, that have blighted this relationship in the past; but simply to enact legislation which alters the nature of proprietary interests in land with the avowed belief that this course of action will, of itself, propagate positive planning, displays governmental naïvety verging upon malfeasance. At this juncture, therefore, it bears repetition to state that the urban land market is a highly complex mechanism where the economic as well as social consequences of radical legislation should be much more fully comprehended before precipitant measures are introduced.

Attempts to define the very nature and function of planning, let alone such refinements as positive, as opposed to what one assumes must be negative, planning, have increasingly appeared to tax the minds of self-accredited 'planning philosophers' over the past decade. There seems to have been little consensus, however, apart from vague moralistic generalizations relentlessly referring, for example, to 'the establishment of community goals', 'the achievement of societal objectives' and 'the promotion of human growth'. Such truisms and hackneyed platitudes do little except to suggest that while planning of some kind performs an undeniably essential collective function in society, it defies the efforts of a particular professional discipline or rigour.

It is suggested that positive planning, by necessity, focusses attention upon implementation, for following McLoughlin: 'the implementation of a plan falls within the general province of control – control as understood in systems engineering and in biological sciences; not in the narrow and restrictive sense of the use of the veto, but in the fullest sense which includes *positive* stimulus and intervention...'[2]

Almost by definition, control in the sense of imparting a positive stimulus requires a full understanding, not only of the system to be controlled and its essential rationale, but perhaps more pertinently of the forces, mechanisms and agencies operating within the system. In this way, the purpose of planning can be moved from its theoretical base of identifying community goals and objectives, and the formulation and evaluation of alternative strategies, to the more prosaic yet more practical stages of realistically comprehending the means by which these goals and objectives can be attained, the likelihood of their achievement, the consequences of their occurrence, and the intervening controls necessary to their fulfilment. These latter stages which together constitute the programme of implementation, are not merely the necessary ingredients of positive planning but also, in a similarly cyclical way to the planning process, contribute a greater understanding of the way in which initial goals and objectives should be drawn up in order to facilitate effective decision-making and, at the same time, give planners a better grasp of the complicated behavioural farrago that in reality constitutes 'the community'.

Returning briefly to the 1974 White Paper on Land, it should be recognized that in labelling the United Kingdom planning system as 'largely negative', it ignores the powers of local authorities to draw up development plans, designate areas for conservation, indicate land for compulsory purchase, prepare design guides, produce planning briefs, enter into partnership schemes, promote housing associations, and execute a wide range of public works. Whilst possibly passive, such initiatives can scarcely be described as negative. Nevertheless, in seeking to remedy the allegedly negative situation, a cumbersome system of conveyancing and re-conveyancing is proposed, and procedures almost designed to produce greater delay and procrastination on the part of local authorities are introduced. Following so closely upon the publication of the Dobry Committee Report on Development Control, these efforts to design a system of positive planning through public ownership and decision-making appear curiously paradoxical.

Structure planning

It is contended in this and subsequent sections that our present system of land-use planning is inappropriate and its endeavours misdirected; our understanding of the workings of private and quasi-public sector land-dealing agencies inadequate; and our present solutions in respect of land policy reforms largely irrelevant.

Since the introduction of the Town and Country Planning Act,

1968, and more especially since the reorganization of local government in 1974, we are faced with a two-tier system of planning – structure plans and local plans – both concerned with the 'development and other use of land'. The scope, form and content of structure plans are set out in detail elsewhere, but the basic functions of structure plans are:[3]

(1) To state and justify, to the public and to the Secretary of State, the authority's policies and general proposals for the development and other use of land in the area concerned (including measures for the improvement of the physical environment and the management of traffic), and thus provide guidance for development (including development control) on issues of structural importance.
(2) To interpret national and regional policies in terms of physical and environmental planning for the area concerned.
(3) To provide the framework and statutory basis for Action Area Plans, which then in turn provide the necessary further guidance for development control at the more detailed local level.

On the face of it, local planning authorities would appear to have become preoccupied with structure planning, to have devoted too many staff and other resources towards the preparation and production of structure plans, and to have become obsessed with the development of esoteric techniques which all too frequently merely provide a refinement in inexactitude. It is possible, although admittedly not proven, that 90 per cent of professional effort is expended to produce the last 10 per cent of strategic solutions.

Although intended to provide a more flexible framework for the execution of planning policy, with a requirement for continuous review and a facility for change, almost the reverse has proved to be the case. At the time of writing (summer 1975), seven years after the 1968 Act and ten after the Planning Advisory Group Report, a number of structure plans have indeed been prepared, but few approved. This in turn automatically implies that few statutory local plans have been formally approved, and consequently the number of semi-official, informal, advisory and even secret local plans has grown out of all proportion, producing the inevitable uncertainty, mistrust and blight. In London alone there are currently fifty-six Action Area Plans drawn up, but none adopted. In terms of its demonstrable contribution to the realization of excessive profits and intensification of the volatile nature of the property market during the early 1970s, the accountability of the planning mechanism with its dubious and ineffectual land-use allocations is rarely raised.

Moreover, even if all structure plans are finally prepared and approved by 1980, it is worth questioning how relevant they will prove in an ever-changing social and economic climate, where increasing instability breeds greater uncertainty in prediction and consequently less reliability upon long-range forecasting. In any event, the intricate web of doubtful statistical evidence would again seem to have nurtured the production of deterministic 'end-state' solutions similar to the 1947 Act format, and appear completely at odds with declared flexibility.

Ever since Churchill declared that 'it is always wise to look ahead, but difficult to look farther than you can see', doubts surrounding the veracity of quantitative statistical forecasts have been voiced. Population predictions, for example, represent the starting point for planning at all scales by setting down guidelines for determining total land resource requirements and giving a basis for allocation between various competing land-use activities. And yet in 1946 the population forecast for the United Kingdom at the turn of the century was placed at between 28 and 44 million, in 1964 it was calculated to reach 73 million, and more recently has been estimated at 64 million. The supposed drift of population to the South East of the country, which dictated so much regional policy during the early 1960s, has been shown to have possessed certain mythical qualities. The target populations of new towns have proved inappropriate, and inconsistent population policies have virtually denuded London of essential service workers. The size, characteristics, distribution and trends in population are collectively but one imponderable in the planning equation. Likely economic performance is naturally another. In the 'never-had-it-so-good' years of the late 1950s, the prospect of doubling the real standard of living within twenty-five years was a credible political promise; the ill-fated National Plan of 1965 indicated the same possibility within fifteen years, but by 1974 we were faced with a predicted no-growth situation for the foreseeable future, and we continue to receive conflicting reports which hazard varying rates and periods of relative growth or decline. Even in more immediate and technically related spheres of policy planning such as transportation, little reliance can be placed upon the precise nature of strategic analysis as the enormous margins of error discovered in the London transportation study befittingly demonstrated. These traits, deficiencies and errors can be traced through all other components in the land-use planning process. Erroneous qualities emerge in housing, leisure, commerce, and energy studies alike, and when the individual inaccuracies are taken and multiplied together, the felony of overfaithfulness to long-term macro-scale planning is compounded.

Notwithstanding the vagaries of future social and economic performance, the value of present adherence to structure planning is further enfeebled by relatively current or short-term changes in public policy. At a national level, the cancellation or substantial amendment of large-scale public works such as a Third London Airport, the Channel Tunnel project, deep-water ports, or motorway programmes, can radically affect the viability of structure plans. A change in policy in respect of land release, industrial investment support or housing subsidies, for example, can again significantly distort their effectiveness. Even relatively arbitrary individual planning decisions – like the grant of planning permission upon appeal of such developments as hypermarkets, conference centres or commercial complexes – can negate the function of a structure plan. At a more local level, where a fiercer respect for prevailing strategic policy might conceivably be expected, the unpredictable fluctuations in political power, combined with the vacillations in planning fashion, all conspire to produce a highly uncertain foundation for future forecasts. The dilatory production of structure plans has also meant that other more partial vehicles of strategic policy have been developed to cope with particularly pressing problems. These include Transport Policies and Programmes, Housing Programmes, Urban Renewal Programmes, Growth Area Policies and Waste Management Plans. Frequently, the policies contained in these alternative strategies conflict with the eventual goals and objectives of the structure plan, thus reducing the efficacy of one or the other, and increasing uncertainty within the planning area concerned. These characteristics are exacerbated by an almost total lack of understanding at all levels of planning of the essential relationship between the structure planning and corporate planning methodologies within local government. In addition, as Solesbury points out,[4] the handling of social impact resource considerations has been disappointing, and the budgetary implications of strategic environmental decision-making are virtually ignored or considered elsewhere. Apart from removing the prejudice of proprietary interest, the generalist nature yet technical expression of structure plans likewise leaves them as poor media for public participation. In many ways, they have been undermined by their own techniques with the means becoming more important than the ends.

Further reservations regarding the relevance of structure planning can be identified in Eversley's succinct aphorism that 'Change and growth are not laws of nature'.[5] Planning has largely evolved its attitudes, techniques and procedures in a post-war climate of expansion, investment and growth. The excessive use of the very term 'development' in respect of 'development plans', 'development control' and 'development areas' neatly makes the point. The structure plan approach and format is essentially an instrument of growth, ill-equipped to manage conditions of stagnation and decline where a redistribution of resources to effect desired community change does not automatically call forth the necessary funds to finance that change. The control and management of land tenure systems remains one of the principal elements in advancing the stewardship of the built environment, and yet the crude panorama portrayed by structure plans is singularly inappropriate to the more sophisticated means of re-ordering land resources likely to be required in the immediate future. The very real possibilities of reduced mobility, economic inertia, the lack of investment funds for innovation, a diminishing demand for industrial development, a falling-off in leisure and recreation opportunities and the advent of an energy crisis all provide illustrations of the way in which the planners' present passive or negative control mechanisms will be weakened, and the type of strategic planning exemplified in prevailing regional, sub-regional and structure plans further invalidated. By the same token, the concentration of concern upon ensuring that future development land passes through public ownership as a relevant reform of land policy in times of no growth, rather than a focussing of attention upon gaining a greater understanding of existing market mechanisms to effect a more efficient reallocation of resources, is but further evidence of misapplied policy thinking.

The above scepticism, which has been recorded without recourse to the fiasco known as the Greater London Development Plan, does not deny the need for some kind of strategic policy, but simply questions the current obsession with pursuing the grand-scale 'master plan' approach, and suggests that with fewer resources to manipulate decisions on the margin become more critical, their economic, social and political consequence greater, and thus the scale of operation essentially more localized. Urban renewal, residential rehabilitation, commercial refurbishment, conscientious structural maintenance, energy conservation, educational priority area programmes, and community development projects, will inevitably supersede the likes of Central Lancashire New Town, Milton Keynes, Strategic Plans for the South East, and the Third London Airport as strategic policies.[6] Having argued that structure plans are altogether too ambitious, however, it is imperative that some form of strategic framework should exist, and should play a more useful role in the planning process, so long as it is confined to a physical, spatial and locational interpretation of wider social and economic policies, based upon a respectively deeper knowledge of both social theory and economic performance.

Local planning

Pursuing the above criticism of structure planning, and the admitted need for some form of overall policy framework, it is suggested that firstly the most beneficial and expedient approach towards a system of strategic planning is a more immediate, flexible, goal-explicit but problem-orientated programme along the lines of an annual local socio-economic position statement – a sort of county-based 'State of the Nation' document, roughly akin to the kind of yearly re-assessment East Sussex proposes. Secondly, that the appropriate vehicle for the proper management of planning areas is the local plan, which readily lends itself to providing a comprehensible expression of changing strategies and sets down a more certain base for appraisal, discussion, participation, negotiation and action.

Designed to apply strategy, give a detailed basis for co-ordination and control of development and bring issues before the public, local plans are already intended to make the new system of development plans more adaptable to changing circumstances. To date, however, we have so few that problems not only persist, but are aggravated by delay and the equivocation of informal plans. It is contended that planning should be more about solving practical problems at a local scale and less about working towards abstract goals in the rarefied atmosphere of strategy. In this context, although the production of structure and local plans should be an iterative process, identifying problems within parochial communities, and incorporating solutions within an overall strategy and taking into account all the attendant trade-offs, there lies a danger in the present system of local planning, whereby local plans follow on the structure plan and can easily become either deterministic devices of it or viewed entirely in isolation.

It is, therefore, advocated that in formulating a viable and effective land policy, the emphasis of the planning process should be firmly placed upon the local scale for the following reasons. Firstly, despite the frequent use of out-of-date methodology and the relatively junior role it occupies in the professional hierarchy, local planning has the potential to furnish the most conducive medium for securing the corporate management of local government activities by pinpointing particular problem areas, and to provide a cogent vehicle for analysis and diagnosis, as well as to supply a serviceable basis for drawing up a programme of action by appropriate organizations within a realistic financial framework, Secondly, local plans bestow ideal opportunities for public participation, being documents and descriptions suitable for discussion and decision on the part of such organizations as community councils, chambers of trade and commerce, residents' associations and action groups, and in doing so assist the land-use planner in not only formulating community policies but in actually identifying the various interest groups involved. Thirdly, a greater accent upon the prompt production of pragmatic local plans could create a milieu more amenable to better urban design, for it is at this level that the domestic and working environment is shaped. Fourthly, in achieving these objectives, the total land and land-use resources of the area, and the respective demands upon them, could be established, enabling local authorities to assess their relative priorities in terms of this scarce commodity. Fifthly, the proper basis for development control would be determined. Sixthly, a means whereby private initiatives could be defined and encouraged would be created. Finally, and perhaps above all, the relative immediacy of local plans and the resultant earlier emergence of measures of performance would increase the accountability of the planning profession. This is important, because land-use planning as an activity requires to be geared towards 'delivering the goods', not restricted to legitimizing the more theoretically abstruse aspects of prevailing planning policy, for as Eddison declaims: 'We are too hidebound by our traditional notions of local plans which, on the whole, add up to cosmetics and Letraset. They are plans constructed by the perspective of the people and machinery preparing them.'[7]

In examining the effectiveness of the existing planning framework, Jones[8] recounts what he describes as a 'parable from planning folk-lore', where a leopard in the jungle, who had been pursued by hunters for many days and could not shake them off, was at his wits' end. Eventually, he sought the King of the Jungle, the Lion, to take his advice. He hurriedly explained what had happened to him and asked: "What must I do to give them the slip?" The Lion thought deeply for many minutes. He then said: "The answer, my boy, is simple. You must change your spots, and then they will not recognize you." The Leopard looked dismayed. "Change my spots?" he queried. "But, Lion, everyone knows a leopard can never change his spots. It's impossible." The Lion looked down at him indignantly and retorted sternly: "My dear chap, as King of the Jungle, I only concern myself with policy; the implementation I leave to you!"

The implementation process

Local plans fall into many categories, but it can be argued that the most appropriate procedure and format for securing the early and effective implementation of planning policy in terms of physical change, whether by development, redevelopment or improvement, are those of the Action Area Plan. This kind of plan relates to areas where 'comprehensive treatment' is required and where, in addition to the usual functions of any local plan, Action Area Plans should explain:

1 The present conditions, problems and prospects of the action area;
2 The strategic framework for the action area as provided by the structure plan;
3 The policies and proposals of the plan;
4 The phasing of any related proposals of the plan;
5 The method of implementation.[9]

Almost as a throw-away line, the Development Plans Manual also stipulates that all the private and public financial implications of the plan should be set out in detail.

The purpose of Action Area Plans, therefore, is not to identify wide social, economic and political issues in abstraction, but rather to resolve more local problems with a greater sense of urgency than has hitherto been the case. Strategic awareness of a broader context is still incumbent upon a planning authority, but Action Area proposals should implicitly relate to an understanding of the implementation process and the overall implications and achievements of the execution of physical change. Once again, however, despite these commendable aspirations, it can be seen that current implementation procedures are rendered inadequate because of the lack of professional and managerial skills on the part of local authorities in their understanding and handling of private sector agencies at the local scale. Furthermore, that a comprehension of the land market, its tenure systems and patterns of value is a vital prerequisite to successful local planning.

Nevertheless, whatever the professional shortcomings, it should also be recognized that the present statutory planning framework provides few special powers of implementation, and that local planning authorities are forced to rely upon the initiatives and activities of existing development agencies. As might be expected, the nature, motives and abilities of these agencies vary considerably. An authoritative taxonomy virtually defies compilation, but the following categorization of implementation agencies provides a useful starting point:

1 *Private development organizations*

This category includes development companies such as Town and City, Land Securities and Capital and County; insurance and pension fund investing institutions like Norwich Union, Legal and General and Electricity Supply Nominees; and large private land-owners such as the Portland and Grosvenor Estates. The common motive of these agencies, who were highly active during the 1960s, is naturally to secure a 'satisfactory' financial return on their assets and investments, although recently they have become more concerned about their image and look for prestigious schemes often incorporating substantial elements of community benefit in order to legitimize and safeguard their activities.

2 *Philanthropic bodies*

These are particularly active in the housing market and are best represented by such organizations as the Guinness Trust, who provide benefit to certain sectors of the community through physical development. It is likely that their role will grow in importance with increasing intervention and taxation in the property market.

3 *Public authorities*

A number of public bodies operating on a quasi-commercial basis, such as British Rail, the National Coal Board, and the Post Office, who are generally interested in maximizing returns in order to offset the rises in cost of providing a public service, have been extremely active in property development over recent years, although they normally have to secure a private Act of Parliament to dispose of land. The respective pension funds of these public bodies have of course displayed even greater development zeal in their capacity within the first category.

4 *Local government*

Several separate situations where local authorities act as an agent of implementation can be identified:

(a) As a commercial developer in their own right, but attempting to ensure that while returns are maximized for the benefit of the ratepayers, they are not done so to the cost of other sections of society.
(b) As part of a statutory duty in respect of such areas as housing, education and highways.
(c) Acting under planning powers to provide facilities for the proper planning of their area such as civic centres, libraries and sports halls.
(d) Developing in another local authority area, as will always be the case with such operations as regional health authorities.

5 *Government department*

These operate either to provide facilities for the execution of their own affairs, or more usually in pursuance of their responsibilities as national authorities in relation to such activities as planning, education and highways.

6 *Others*

A host of other agencies such as private firms, builders and individual landowners, naturally contribute to the implementation of planning policy, and while their characteristics vary, their motives generally remain the same – those of self-interest.

As referred to previously, positive planning implies implementation, and implementation implies control. The control mechanisms available to local authorities can be summarized as follows:

1 Development control procedures and conservation powers under Parts III to V of the Town and Country Planning Act of 1971.
2 Negotiation with development agencies, often assisted by the use of planning briefs and ending in some kind of informal agreement, a conditional planning permission or a formal agreement under Section 52 of the 1971 Act.

3 Control through formal and informal inter-governmental relationships.
4 Contractual control with developers by means of leasehold arrangements.
5 Special enabling powers conferred by Private Act of Parliament.
6 Control exercised by local authorities over their own schemes.

The relative occurrence and effectiveness of these respective controls naturally varies according to the particular land-use activity concerned, the development agency engaged and the local authority involved. The nature of development control, however, is essentially passive, if not actually negative. Of itself, it rarely promotes, facilitates or expedites desired local authority development, remaining a reaction to initiatives made elsewhere. Despite the growing use of development briefs and planning guidelines relating to particular sites and setting down local planning authority views on such elements as land-use, density, access, height, materials, open space and parking, it remains that in the final analysis an authority can only judge an application for planning permission on the basis of 'can it be refused on proper planning grounds?' rather than 'can a better solution be found?'[10] Although the existence of guidelines and briefs, together with subsequent negotiations between parties, frequently achieves limited improvements in the quality of development schemes, they are only as potent as the local authority's ability to refuse planning permission and the strength of their arguments at appeal. One of the major problems that has resulted from this situation is that at a time of uncertain markets, high interest rates and escalating building costs, administrative delay, or the prospect thereof, becomes a most powerful negotiating instrument to local planning authorities, albeit a highly unsatisfactory and cynical one. As will be seen in Chapter 8 on Partnership, even agreements to regulate the development of land under Section 52 of the 1971 Act, which themselves follow private sector development initiatives, can only be entered into voluntarily; in addition to which the position regarding positive covenants binding successors in title has still not been fully clarified.

A simple dichotomy is often distinguished between private development on the one hand and public planning on the other. The stage of implementation in planning is much more of an imbroglio than such a clear cut conflict would, however, suggest. As Friend and Jessop maintain,[11] planning issues and decisions are not merely a function of the 'process' of planning alone, but are affected and governed by the entire framework within which planning operates. This framework in turn possesses an assemblage of actors, some of whom are participants within the actual process and some, though playing roles outside it, significantly influence results. The two-tier system of local government planning ideally illustrates the enigmas of this concept. While a theoretical logic can be made out for separating the respective powers at strategic and local level, two probable outcomes can be discerned – delay and disagreement. The interminable consultations conducted as between county and district, or Greater London Council and constituent London Borough, taken together with the manifest political and professional dissension that pervades local government in general, contributes little to improving the prospects of establishing effective implementation procedures.

A further, and probably more profound, dimension, which detracts from the autonomy of local planning authorities in managing the implementation of their own plan is the role, relationship and accountability of other exogenous agencies. Putting aside the private landowner, investment institutions and development companies, there are a multitude of other public or quasi-public bodies involved in most major planning decisions. Possibly the most prominent of these agencies is the Department of the Environment, and, to a lesser extent, the Department of Trade and Industry, the Treasury and other government departments. Collectively central government retains considerable powers regarding development plan approval, compulsory purchase, availability of finance, regional policy, trunk road and motorway programmes, overall housing policy, national transport industries and the like; not to mention the plethora of orders, circulars, directives, policy notes and other statutory instruments which emerge from time to time. At a slightly more local level, such other bodies as gas, electricity and water authorities; rail, air, train, water and road transport undertakings; regional and area health authorities; police and traffic commissioners, all possess planning and implementation powers. Not only do they exercise these powers in respect of development at large, but many of them are substantial land-dealing agencies in their own right, and are often protected by a privileged planning position. Another factor which habitually affects the implementation of planning proposals is the policy of neighbouring authorities. The decision, by an adjoining authority, for example, to permit out-of-town shopping within the curtilage of its own area may well have serious and far-reaching repercussions upon the level and pattern of retailing in the area concerned, and thereby invalidate its own shopping proposals. It can be seen, therefore, that the autonomous powers of local authorities to actually plan and ensure that proposed plans reach fruition according to given programmes are severely limited.

Planning gain

The arguments surrounding the recoupment of community created values have already been well rehearsed. In the context of planning, however, land is the key, for it is the physical development or improvement which takes place on land as a consequence of the implementation of planning policy which releases the financial benefits resulting from the investment decision and the planning permission. Because the financial benefits produced by private development schemes cannot be recouped by local authorities, except directly from increased rate revenue and indirectly by central government recycling of taxes on development profits, they have been forced to resort to extracting physical gains on behalf of the community. These development 'tithes' have taken many forms. For example, assistance with public transport systems, road improvements, construction of public services and utilities, restoration of historic buildings, tree planting, landscaping, inclusion of open space, demolition of unsightly buildings, erection of pedestrian walkways, reclamation of derelict land, outright gift of commercial premises and, perhaps most popularly, the provision of residential accommodation either by way of council housing on the development site or private housing sometimes with local authority nomination of a proportion of tenants. It is in connection with the last category that the product of planning gain has been described as probably putting the wrong use, in the wrong place, at the wrong time, for the wrong people, at the wrong price for possibly the right reason.

Despite the sudden vogue for playing the planning gain game, it should not be thought that the inherent negotiation and 'trade-off' situation subsisting between developers and planning authorities is new. It has certainly existed in one form or another since the Second World War, and it is worth remembering that a large number of partnership schemes over the last twenty years, particularly with town centre redevelopment, have proved both socially acceptable and mutually beneficial. Admittedly the scales in the past appear to have tipped in favour of the private sector, partly because of the negative nature and limited effect of planning powers, partly because of the lack of proper entrepreneurial competition and partly because of insufficient expertise within local authorities.

The current impetus to the concept of planning gain has been accelerated by the Greater London Council's decree that all development schemes which include a significant office floor-space content should demonstrate certain planning advantages. This policy has been strengthened by the independent action of individual London Boroughs, who have contrived indices or ratios relating permitted commercial floor-space to required residential accommodation. Results vary from parity to a ratio of 5:1 in favour of housing, but average out at about 2:1. A tenuous relationship in any event, but a good position to begin bargaining.

While applauding the increased combativeness of local authorities in their dealings with the private development sector, certain reservations as to the present practice and future role of planning gain transactions are appropriate in an examination of land policy and the performance of planning. Firstly, there has been an alarming incidence of planning departments seeking to enforce what amount to illegal, *ultra vires*, or invalid conditions upon the grant of planning permission. Secondly, the planning gain is generally limited in location to the development site in question – which may not be suitable for the purpose proposed, or might involve the local planning authority in amending their plans if it seemed that this was the only opportunity of securing the particular benefit. Certainly, the *ad hoc* incorporation of housing and other public facilities within commercial development projects is likely to conflict with comprehensive and cohesive planning. Thirdly, the planning gain may well be a development gain in disguise. For instance, the provision of a bus terminal or the inclusion of a multi-storey car park as part of a shopping scheme, both of which represent actual planning gain transactions, increases accessibility, catchment, turnover and therefore profit. Fourthly, criticisms regarding the dilatory workings of the planning machine are legion and further unwarranted delay over unreasonable haggling will only serve to aggravate the situation, while at the same time reducing the feasibility and even the likelihood of desired development, thus forsaking the possibility of any gain to anyone. Fifthly, the planning gain proposed may not be an urgent requirement of the community and might, therefore, be a waste of scarce resources. It is often the case that local authority planners actually experience some difficulty in identifying a realistic planning gain, because of the constraints of the site, which again results in further delays. Sixthly, the arbitrary nature by which the planning gain game rules are applied, varying, as they do, not only from area to area but from case to case, could easily make dissident demands for community benefits synonymous with uncertainty, and therefore discourage the participation of private sector agencies all together. Finally, the local authority may, in some cases, be placed in the invidious position of effectively 'trading' in planning permissions, thereby producing a conflict of interest which may result in undesirable social repercussions.

Despite considerable variations of interpretation and practice there is little doubt that most development agencies accept the inevitability, if not equity, of the imposition of planning gain, and are increasingly prepared to demonstrate some element of community benefit in their proposals. At the same time there is a danger that the planners' display of social enterprise could give way to public intransigence. But somehow it all misses the point. What is required are appropriate planning frameworks and procedures, not partial short-term palliatives.[12]

References

1 N. Moor, 'Planning and the Market', *Journal of the Town Planning Institute*, January 1970.

2 J. McLoughlin, *Urban and Regional Planning – A Systems Approach*, Faber, 1969.

3 Department of the Environment, *Development Plans – A Manual on Form and Content*, 1970.

4 W. Solesbury, 'Ideas About Structure Plans', *Town Planning Review*, July 1975.

5 D. Eversley, 'Planning in an Age of Stagnation', *Built Environment*, January 1975.

6 *ibid.*

7 T. Eddison, *Local Government: Management and Corporate Planning*, Leonard Hill, 1973.

8 K. Jones, unpublished diploma thesis, Polytechnic of Central London, 1975.

9 Department of the Environment, *op. cit.*

10 Jones, *op. cit.*

11 J. Friend and W. Jessop, *Local Government and Strategic Choice*, Tavistock Institute, 1969.

12 J. Ratcliffe, 'Planning Gain is not the Answer', *Built Environment*, March 1974.

7 Development

In defining the verb 'to develop' as bringing or coming from a latent to an active or visible state, the *Oxford English Dictionary* neatly illustrates the propinquity between the private sector development process and the implementation of public planning policy. In further construing 'development' as a 'gradual unfolding', it is also identifies the more doubtful aspect of its nature. Although reference will be made to public sector development, this chapter is largely concerned with the private sector of the development industry and the role, relationship and future it possesses with regard to the framing and execution of a coherent national land policy.

The emergence of the property development industry as a major force in the national economy largely dates from the Second World War, pre-war conditions being such that they actively discouraged the private property developer. The period of economic recession during the 1920s and 1930s witnessed the least inflationary conditions of the century. There were, in fact, few property concerns as such, for commercial and industrial companies tended to build their own factories and lease their office accommodation from the great landed estates. If let, property was usually held on long leases at fixed rents with ground rents proving to be the most popular form of investment.

During the Second World War, however, some 3 250 000 properties were either damaged or destroyed, producing a situation where effective demand for accommodation of all kinds vastly outstripped potential supply. The initial response by the development industry was severely constrained by inadequate war-damage payments, building licence control, shortage of materials, restricted borrowing facilities and the 100 per cent development charge introduced by the 1947 Town and Country Planning Act. Nevertheless, despite the impediments, a considerable amount of reconstruction work was undertaken in the immediate post-war years, often by means of lessor schemes, whereby a developer who identified a possible development site would submit a scheme to the then Ministry of

Works, who would in turn seek an appropriate government user for the site, and put the two parties together. Such schemes worked tolerably well at the time, but as the government departments concerned would only take a long lease at a fixed rent, the absence of rent revision clauses soon rendered the arrangement unattractive as economic growth and inflation gained momentum.

Despite continuing credit control, the abolition of the development charge in 1953 and the lifting of building licence control in 1954 have jointly been described as lifting the floodgates for commercial property development. The boom which took off during the 1950s was accelerated by a change in funding methods, for whereas building societies had traditionally provided finance for development, their role became largely restricted, both by choice and by statute, to the financing of the owner-occupied residential sector and developers were first forced to look to the major construction companies for assistance and then increasingly to the great financial institutions. The advent of the sale-and-leaseback transaction, described below, between developers and institutions, provided a further surge in activity and a 'new era' of agreements began.

Naturally, the level and pattern of property investment is closely related to the overall investment market, but it was not until the late 1950s and early 1960s that property development companies had any startling effect on the Stock Exchange. In 1958, for example, the number of deals in property shares was 16 000, but within a year it had risen to 102 000 and by 1962 to 184 000. A similar and related growth in the number of quoted property companies was also experienced. Despite, or more probably because of, the general economic uncertainty of the 1960s, investment in property continued to grow with the institutions burgeoning forth in their roles as both financiers and partners. Between 1961 and 1971, insurance companies alone increased their stake in property from £1035 million to £3357 million, or, put another way, from 15 per cent of their total holdings to over 20 per cent. At the same time, confidence in the industry grew to such a level that a phenomenon known as the *reverse yield gap* appeared with property development and investment yields falling below fixed interest securities. This was accompanied by a succession of additional statutory constraints and impositions upon the property market, some of which, like the 1964 ban on office development, produced unforeseen regressive results. The market continued to gather pace through the late 1960s and early 1970s, until the autumn of 1973, when, as a result of a general cash-flow crisis in the industry, the machinery of development was thrown into reverse and the entire nature, function, performance, and future of the development process has been called into question.

The function of development

Despite the obvious drawbacks of a market system, whereby poor consumers are disadvantaged, the production of apparently non-profitable goods and services is discouraged and the incidence of externalities is not accounted for, such a mechanism can be said to have a number of 'saving graces'. In most circumstances, it stimulates innovation, encourages efficiency, rations and re-allocates scarce resources, and, because of its demand-orientated perspective, is mindful of consumer preference. Additionally, in the particular context of the development process, it facilitates funding, promotes expertise and provides a test of feasibility.

In giving a tangible measure of opportunity cost, the market makes a valuable contribution to the introduction of a public authority inspired site leasehold system of estate management, for although the resulting rents need not be pitched at open market levels, it is nevertheless important to know what those levels are. In any event, a self-regulating system is preferable to one which constantly requires administrative intervention, correction and control, and although the equilibrium to which self-regulation adjusts in unfettered conditions might not be socially acceptable, the aim of intervention in a mixed economy should be the construction of a framework which induces the self-regulating market mechanism to achieve societal equilibria.

A further advantage conferred by open market operations is that the inherent demand pressures can provide guidelines for planning policy, and prevailing rents and values offer a monitoring device, albeit partial, of policy performance. Such economic guidelines can also be employed as social indicators, although it should be noted that because of the nature of many public goods, the incidence of externalities, the subconscious reference to historical prices, the uneven distribution of income, and the dearth of market information, great care must be exercised in their use.

In extolling the virtues of private sector agencies as instruments of public policy, a further note of caution requires introduction. The activities of the development process operating within the market system does not automatically imply the existence of a *free* market.

The current fragmented pattern of private ownership in land and property, the rigidity of supply imposed by the finite nature of land, the multiplicity of statutory and administrative controls, the magnitude of investment, the financial power exercised by a group of private institutions, all underpinned by the confidence of the Stock Exchange, collectively contribute to what is fast becoming an oligopolistic situation. One, moreover, where greater power is exercised by the development agencies than by the planning authorities. The situation is frequently reinforced, and even exacerbated, by ill-conceived or misplaced policy measures designed to ameliorate speculative inflationary tendencies but, through a lack of understanding market forces and an inability to extrapolate economic and social repercussions, they actually rebound upon society and its strategic planning objectives. In some of their manifestations rent control legislation, leasehold enfranchisement, office and industrial development control, general improvement area policy, green belt designation and even Parker-Morris standards and the Housing Cost Yardstick all exemplify this short-coming.

As a result of its role in post-war tertiary sector expansion, the property market has acquired incomparable expertise in urban development portfolio management. This has not only been obtained in exclusively private sector investments, but also in respect of large-scale central area mixed development schemes either separate from, or in conjunction with, local authorities. It is paradoxical that the larger the scheme, the greater has become the need for private sector participation. This is not merely confined to negotiating, funding, construction, letting and management aspects, but is commonly directed at 'putting it all together'. The development function is, after all, essentially a co-ordinating function, perhaps paradoxically again, though in a limited management sense only, a 'planning' function. Primarily, however, the distinguishing feature of the private sector process of development is that it preserves the opportunity of choice.

The development process

Just as planning is theoretically described as a rational decision-making process, so too the development process can be said to possess an inherent logic or rationale. A similar cycle from goal formulation through the setting up of objectives, generation of alternative strategies, their evaluation, selection and implementation, to the monitoring, review and feedback of initial goals can be discerned. Naturally enough, however, the principal goal in the private sector is invariably one of profit maximization, although related ones of liquidity, security and prestige play an increasingly prominent part in the development decision. The process of development is obviously more partial than that of planning. It is, nevertheless, a component of it, emerging fully at the stage of implementation and determining the degree of effective execution of public policy. In this way, the relationship between the process of planning and development can be likened to two dependent cogs meshing in the mechanism of urban change. It is, therefore, contended that an understanding of the path of development and the attributes of the various contributing agencies is essential to the establishment of an effective land policy and the propagation of efficient planning implementation.

There can in reality be no exhaustive or authoritative classification of the process of development, for, due to the heterogeneous nature of the land market, the range of development situations is almost infinite. The following description, however, serves to illustrate the series of steps involved. The first step can be described as *site identification*, which attempts to match the goals of the development organization with the supply of land given the constraints of finance, expertise, experience and market demand. The search will include developed and undeveloped land and will be cast over a wide geographic area, wider than that permitted to individual local authorities. Frequently a selection of sites and opportunities will be supplied to a developer by estate agents. It is at this initial stage that the special intuition and flair of the private developer is displayed, for the ability to visualize substantial change and at the same time grasp unique opportunities for action would seem to be a predominantly private-sector trait.

Once a site has been identified, then almost immediately the second step of *preliminary appraisal* is embarked upon. Such information as is available regarding local conditions of demand, prevailing planning policies, future proposals for the area, rental levels and costs of construction are assembled and subsequently analysed by means of a simple residual valuation to determine in principle whether or not further steps are worth pursuing. The necessary market evidence is freely accessible to private agencies who operate on a wider basis than local authorities, and who maintain a network of formal and informal contacts from which information can be more readily obtained. Recently, however, local government has resorted to retaining professional consultants for advice in respect of commercial development propositions.

If the preliminary appraisal proves positive, an *outline programme* will be drawn up. This will consider the possible timing of the scheme, the resources in terms of money and manpower required to effect it, and the appropriate management structure for the operation. It is at about this stage in the process that one of the main attributes of the private sector can be discerned. Decisions can be made with a minimum of prevarication and delay. Amendments to original plans can be allowed for with the suitable degree of urgency so essential to economic performance. Rightly or wrongly, corporate or committee based decisions in the public sector are beset by conflicting interests, and all too often produce an acceptable solution based upon the path of least resistance reflecting the lowest common factors involved.

The next step in the process is the commissioning of a *detailed investigation* of the physical, economic, legal and social parameters of development, This will include a survey of the site to identify any inherent physical problems regarding topography, geology, underground workings and architectural and historic remains. The availability and terms of finance, the local demand for space and the presence of other competitors will be fully scrutinized. Architects will be instructed to prepare outline designs, so that in conjunction with quantity surveyors and structural engineers a broad picture of costs can be obtained. A legal search relating to land title and the possible existence of any restrictive covenants will be conducted. Discussions will be held with the relevant authorities regarding the provisions of services, the need and availability of office development permits and industrial development certificates, and the general requirements of the planning authority. Following these discussions, a more detailed financial appraisal, taking account of other fiscal implications, can be constructed again and a decision to proceed or not can be taken.

If the auguries are still favourable, *site assembly* will commence following the necessary agreements with the funding institutions. This part of the process could entail either the complicated piecing together of many varying interests in one or many plots of land or the single negotiation with an individual freeholder for the purchase of the sole interest in one site. It can also involve the taking of options on land consequent upon the obtaining of planning permission and total land assembly. Some or all of the acquisitions might conceivably have been made at an earlier stage in the process. Although the argument is often advanced that local authorities, through their powers of compulsory purchase, have a distinct advantage in the assembling of sites, the constraints imposed by the present economic climate have severely restricted their activities in this direction. Moreover, even where development is publicly devised, many councils are increasingly being forced to rely upon private sector acquisition, occasionally backed up by the threat of compulsory purchase where individual opposition or intransigence is encountered. At around this stage in the process application for planning permission is normally made. In the public sector, it usually precedes site assembly, and in the private sector it is frequently made afterwards.

The next step of *choosing the final professional team* is one where the scope afforded to private sector development agencies unquestionably surpasses that of the public sector. Private institutions and companies can select the most suitable architect, quantity surveyor, structural engineer, builder, lawyer and agent for individual schemes. Some have specialist skills with which to overcome particular problems and can be judged according to their previous track record or performance. It is also easier in private practice to make changes in the professional team if required. In the municipal sector, however, local authorities are often expected to employ their own professional officers on development schemes wherever possible, and it is inevitable that on the whole their experience is more limited, and arguably that their motivation for expediting the work less immediate. Additionally, private developer companies usually appoint their own project manager, the most important member of the team, whose responsibility it is to supervise and co-ordinate the efforts of the other members of the team, according to his proven worth and peculiar skills. In some development organizations, this function is divided between a development controller, often an estate manager, whose work load predominantly occurs during those stages before planning permission is obtained and after the development nears completion; and a project manager, who could be an architect, engineer or quantity surveyor, who is largely concerned with on-site operations during the contract and construction period. Nevertheless, although many variations of management structure exist, the point remains that greater flexibility, expedition and accountability exist in the private sector. Municipal authorities are all too often bedevilled by inter-departmental rivalry and disorder.

After the selection and appointment of the professional team, the *contract stage* is reached, following which the *construction process* begins as soon as possible. The two stages are roughly similar in both public and private sectors, although tendering is still very much more common in local authority sponsored situations. The final stages after the completion of the development are *management and disposition*, which will in fact have begun at an earlier stage in the development process with a letting campaign and all the attendant advertising, publicity and negotiation. A management scheme containing such items as the proper tenant mix, rental levels, repair and maintenance review periods, security, tenant associations and rent collection, will also have been drawn up. A decision will also be made as to whether the completed development will remain in the developer's portfolio as an investment or will be sold to release capital funds for further development. Again, the experience gained by the private sector in the fields of marketing, property management and investment analysis is vastly superior to that of local government.

Finance for development

Given subsisting demand, any successful development depends upon two basic ingredients, professional expertise and proper financing. At the time of writing, the property development industry has experienced a 'rationalization' of the first through a deficiency of the second. The market, however, appears to be recovering from the traumas of the past few years and the following brief description of financing methods in reality represents what has been and what might be again. It is included in the text to illustrate further the flexible nature and relative sophistication of the private sector, and thus the need to maintain a mixed economy approach towards land and development policy.

Two distinct requirements for finance can be identified in property development. Firstly, short- and medium-term finance, which are required to fund a project from initiation to completion at which juncture, if an interest is to be retained, the second facility for long-term finance needs to be arranged.

Apart from that proportion provided by the individual developer, short-term finance is normally supplied by *joint stock banks, merchant banks* and *finance houses*. The activities of the joint stock banks, who tend to charge a rate of interest 3 to 7 per cent above base rate, have been curtailed by the Bank of England. In any event, with an absence of equity participation in development projects, their attitude has always been somewhat conservative. Even in circumstances where they are prepared to make advances, they usually restrict loans to between 60 and 80 per cent of development value. Such loans are also liable to be called in at short notice, and the developer is generally required to give personal guarantees as collateral. Over the past ten to fifteen years, the bulk of short-term funding has increasingly been undertaken by merchant banks, and more recently during the very early 1970s by the more dubious 'secondary banking' sector. Although the facilities afforded by merchant banks to developers vary one to another, the arrangement usually defines the maximum amount available; lays down the period for which it is available, rarely being more than five years; retains the bank's right to approve projects and obliges the developer to offer certain other projects he might entertain to the bank; stipulates the rate of interest, generally around 5 per cent over inter-bank rate; agrees a rolling-up provision for interest payment, either for the financial facility as a whole or for particular projects; establishes the bank's right to revalue the relevant parts of the development company's portfolio assets in respect of continued security; and reflects the negotiated equity sharing arrangement, usually between 30 and 40 per cent in respect of the bank. Some of the more disreputable fringe banks have in the past sought a 51 per cent dividend in a scheme and, at the first signs of trouble, have insisted upon stepping in and taking over operations. Another source of short-term funds have been the large well-established public property companies who have often set up a joint company in conjunction with smaller developers who may possess flair, initiative, skill and, above all, a good scheme. Such an arrangement will normally permit the individual developer to retain the major share of the equity while the public company preserve the rights of approval, financial control and possibly take-up options.

The major source of long-term finance comes from the institutions, that is, the large insurance companies and pension funds, and more recently the property unit trusts and property bonds. One of the principal devices by which arrangements are effected is the *sale-and-leaseback* which has largely replaced the straightforward *mortgage*. Basically, the sale-and-leaseback involves the disposal of the freehold or long leasehold in the development by the developer to an institution for a capital sum in return for a lease being granted back.

Generally, the property is sold at full market value in which case the leaseback rent is fixed at the prevailing rack rent with customary reviews. Occasionally properties are sold at less than market value with the leaseback rental reduced to reflect the difference. The main reason why property development companies have resorted to the use of sale-and-leaseback is the manifestation of the reverse yield gap whereby, as previously described, equity holdings have produced lower yields than government stock and, more specifically with property, interest rates for borrowing have risen above property yields. Moreover unlike the ordinary mortgage which is normally confined to a proportion of market value, the leaseback enables the developer to realize the full value of the property. A number of refinements to the conventional sale-and-leaseback arrangement have emerged over the last few years, such as the *horizontal leaseback*, otherwise known as the 'top-slice' leaseback, where the developer is placed in a subordinate ungeared position regarding rental income with the institution assured of an agreed figure, and the developer relying on the riskier but potentially remunerative top slice; the *vertical leaseback*, otherwise known as the side-by-side leaseback, where the institution and the property company share the equity of development in agreed proportion, the developer thereby avoiding the vulnerability of top-slice income and the institution providing for possible growth in profits; and the *reverse leaseback*, whereby the institution agrees to purchase a long-lease and sub-lets back enabling the developer to retain the freehold and therefore the assured and marketable bottom slice of income.

The other methods of raising long-term finance include *internal financing* where capital is generated from within a company by the sale of existing assets. Again, this recourse has been dictated by the existence of the reverse yield gap with mortgages costing around 12 to 14 per cent and first-class development returns producing between 5 and 8 per cent. Consequently many property companies have sought to make good the shortage of development finance at economic rates of interest by stimulating internal cash flows through disposition of existing properties from their portfolio or by developing for immediate sale, thus avoiding the need for end money. A further long-term alternative source of finance is by way of *share issue*, and, while property development companies generally try to avoid making rights issues in their own equity, with mortgage and debenture interest rates running at exceptionally high levels, many have found it necessary to resort to this method. The last and currently least popular means of financing development schemes are therefore the raising of *mortgage* and *debenture* capital. When conversion factors, that is the relationship between value and cost, were high, as in the 1960s, there was no great disadvantage to employing this approach, but in the present climate, where even negative values prevail, they are largely rejected as funding instruments.

It can, therefore, be seen that varying economic circumstances produce a range of appropriate reactions on the part of development agencies in respect of the financing of property development, and that the negotiations, understandings and relationships that persist between funding institutions and development companies are carefully established, highly sophisticated and finely balanced. Additionally, the amounts involved are of a very significant magnitude. In the light of the need for these complex agreements, considerable caution should be exercised when interfering with private sector funding procedures and replacing them by crude and paradoxically short-term public sector budgetary arrangements. The property development industry represents one of the largest fields of investment in the economy, and apart from supplying shelter, it provides the raw space materials for the pursuance of trade and industry, and yet, none the less, a conflict rages around the role of land and property development within society.

The conflict

The partial, piecemeal and proprietary nature of the urban land market, and the pecuniary motivation of its private sector agencies, remain anathema to the planner. Equally, the utopian unrealities of abstract planning policies, plagued with blight and debilitated by procedural delay, produce intense cynicism on the part of the development industry and the self-accredited professions of the land. Nevertheless, both planning and market mechanisms are occupied with determining the optimum use of land, albeit from differing standpoints. Land in this way has become the battleground but the causes of conflict between what should be the complementary processes of planning and development are infinitely more intricate than a mere dichotomy over land tenure systems and the distribution of the dividends from development.

To begin with, a basic misunderstanding arises from the difference between planning need and market demand. Correctly, the planning function is community and welfare orientated, attempting to ameliorate unacceptable conditions in society, establish appropriate standards, predict and provide for future requirements and generally improve environmental amenity. It does not, however, possess the means by which these goals can be attained, nor does it always equate future aspirations with present feasibility. Moreover, the development industry operating in a freer market economy, and gearing its level of production to prevailing demand and supply conditions, is frequently concerned with preserving high levels of scarcity and thus demand. Likewise, the market demand for certain activities may well be high, such as that for out-of-town shopping, but public sector interpretation of social need may not necessarily be in accord. Put another way, planning is occupied with goal maximization, whereas the development industry is primarily concerned with the maximization of profits.

From this basic divergence of interest stem several other sources of contention. A preoccupation with goal identification and achievement on the part of the planning profession naturally produces a general understanding of the social system, the intricate pattern of social relations, the need for particular social services, the protection of minority interests, and the overall desires, demands, priorities and problems of individuals or groups within a community. Laudable enough objectives in themselves, but incomplete without a thoroughgoing knowledge of the related parallel economic system. Equally, the development industry, while preserving a deep understanding of the forces and agencies operating within the economic system, pays scant regard to the wider social repercussions of its location and operational decisions. Although this portrays an admittedly polarized situation, it is nevertheless suggested that greater accent should be placed by the public planning sector upon the comprehension of economic constraints and performance, perhaps by a greater use of property and development consultants, and more attention paid by the private sector development industry to the social effects of its activities, possibly along the lines of preparing impact studies as a prerequisite to an application for planning permission, as recommended by the recent Dobry Report on Development Control. In this context, it is noticeable that the most common accusation levelled at the development industry is that its speculative operations attract investment funds that would otherwise have been directed into more 'productive' areas of general industry and commerce. The charge, however, is simplistic. Commercial organizations of all complexions employ their property assets not merely for actual productive operations but also as collateral for securing further investment funds. Property assets account for approximately 40 per cent of total fixed company assets held by private sector companies, and with bank lending to industry running at over £16 000 million a year, it is reasonable to surmise that if direct loans to property companies, which account for about £2700 million, are excluded, and if advances are secured in proportion to fixed asset structure, something in the region of at least £5000 million of industrial and commercial funds can be vicariously attributed to property. The movement towards leasehold tenure on the part of industry is also releasing further capital funds for reinvestment. Whatever the circumstances, this dual lack of percipience continues to result in a mutual distrust of motives.

One of the most obvious manifestations of this distrust is seen in the bureaucratic label which is so often attached to the planning profession. Even other professions of the land working within local government frequently tag town planners with epithets surrounding the general theme of 'unrealistic and misguided social dreamers'. Such criticism is perhaps inevitable, for, as Muchnick points out,[1] planners are primarily occupied with what he describes as the politico-strategic level of government and not much so with the managerial or executive levels, and, apart from their development control responsibilities, are rarely involved in the implementation of their policies, a task more usually left to other departments. Dealing in such subjective fields, the planner often appears as dogmatic and ideological, a reaction more recently reinforced by the advent of the 'bureaucratic guerilla' – the extreme political activist disguised as professional planner prepared to further his own philosophical predilections at whatever cost to other community considerations. The argument can also be advanced that planning barely justifies the designation 'profession', because, using the normal classification for delineating professional work, it lacks the necessary professional autonomy, retains a remarkably tenuous professional-client relationship and possesses a much disputed professional authority or respect. The hodge-podge miscellany of social science and quasi-technical training that has become planning might, if mixed with management skills, be an essential corporate activity but it defies identification as an individual discipline. The probity of such strictures is illustrated by the nature of planning education which, with its broad horizons and comprehensive perspective, produces a veritable plethora of comparatively well-informed laymen who increasingly appear to know less and less about more and more. Additionally, the quality, commitment and accountability of local government staff is often challenged, and undeniably, as in any bureaucracy where there is really no 'hire and fire' basis of employment, there are bound to be degrees of inefficiency and abuse. It is not always recognized, however, particularly by private development agencies, that the working climate, context and terms of reference of the respective processes are fundamentally different.

Conversely, the other side of the coin reveals to many planners a development industry motivated by greed, steeped in speculation, staffed by furtive entrepreneurs and marshalled by a landed profession deeply sunk in abject cynicism. The very operation of development is veiled in unnecessary secrecy and initial developers' demands are usually boasted to explore and capitalize upon any planning weaknesses. This mutual distrust is further exacerbated by the frustration caused to both planning and development organizations by the external decisions of other bodies and agencies, the inherent delays and dilatoriness persisting in the public sector decision-making process, and the arbitrary nature of political decisions at all levels repeatedly negating professional negotiations, understandings and recommendations. The gulf is a wide one and continues to threaten the future functioning of both public planning and private development.

The future for private development

A cynic might declaim that with the introduction of the Community Land Act there is little or no future for private development. Conversely, and more positively, it should be recognized that there is no chance of the Community Land Act working without the contribution of the private sector property development industry. In many ways, if the Act is applied with the utmost discretion by local authorities, or in other words largely ignored, the development industry could assume as important a role as ever. The slump in the market since 1973 and the related decline in values may confer hidden benefits for the future. The buccaneers and simple speculators have been largely found out, the weakest development companies have gone to the wall, the false and dangerous optimism of the early 1970s has disappeared, the financial foolishness of the institutions and the malfeasance of the secondary banking sector are unlikely to be repeated, and those development agencies which remain active will now retain a more becoming commercial caution in their operations. In the meantime, local planning authorities and their professional staff have gained experience and become slightly more adroit in their dealings with developers. Thus, there remains a future role for the private developer who can still supply a certain degree of initiative, flair, special knowledge, enterprise, risk-bearing, co-ordination, management and marketing abilities of a calibre which are rarely to be found in local government. Local government, however, can in turn concentrate upon its functions of intervention, stimulus and control in effecting proper planning policy.

In the same way that the previous chapter called for a change in prevailing planning procedures, so too with the development process and development agencies. Firstly, there is a need to sponsor much greater research into the characteristics and determinants of the urban land market. Development decisions are increasingly being made on the margin and a higher degree of certainty as to the nature and performance of all the elements of the development process is required. To ensure this, the use of new techniques is desirable. Whereas the planning profession might have become befuddled with a host of novel methodologies, the development professions are strangely conservative in their adoption of new techniques or their adaption to existing ones. It is always surprising to other professions involved in financial appraisal, for example, when valuers display a marked reluctance to employ simple discounted cash flow analysis to explore investment decisions, let alone statistical techniques such as sensitivity analysis and probability distribution to examine the components of risk and uncertainty. Again in sharp contrast to planning, even short-term forecasting is virtually unknown in the surveying professions, and, while grave doubts can be cast at the over-reliance upon predictive models, some form of plotting future patterns of demand, labour and materials as well as financial performance needs to be established.

Growing public awareness coupled with increased devolution of political power will surely demand a new development ethic. To mitigate the consequences of the conflict previously described, development agencies will be further required to demonstrate degrees of community benefit and social responsibility in all their activities. Escalating infrastructure costs will also dictate a more economically realistic approach to development at all scales because the combination of the Community Land Act and Development Land Tax will mean that the private developer will be unable to carry high initial costs.[2] Programming of infrastructure provision will therefore need to be more effective, and once again a closer rapport between planner and developer achieved.

Inevitably, the introduction of the Community Land Act will fundamentally change the respective roles of the participating parties to the development process. With more and more land passing through public ownership, that portion of development value that pertains to the profit element of land will disappear and only the returns from construction will remain. The likely result of this loss of development profit is that private development agencies at best will be extremely reluctant to assemble prospective sites before planning permission is obtained, and, at worst, will take the view that insufficient margins of profit exist to justify undertaking particular schemes. Moreover, in the context of land assembly, the legislation provides inadequate guarantees to potential developers who, having pieced a site together, could easily find it compulsorily acquired and disposed of to another development agency. In this way, uncertainty is increased and the necessary risk-bearing return correspondingly rises, further aggravating the situation. It is also worth remembering that one of the prime generators of the private sector development industry is institutional finance, and the growing control of land ownership exercised by the large financial institutions has been one of the most significant features of the land market over the past decade. It is currently very difficult to anticipate the reaction of the institutions to the changing political climate. It is, however, possible that with many other alternative avenues for investment, they could well adopt an extremely cautious approach towards future property development opportunities. In any event, public authorities will find the strength of the larger institutions, combined with their relative political protection, a much tougher proposition to deal with in direct partnership negotiations than is the case with smaller, more overtly competitive individual property developers.

A possible future role for the established property company is that of development consultant to local authorities working on a retained fee basis as opposed to equity remuneration. The developer, as opposed to the speculator who merely trades in interests in land, has accumulated considerable expertise as a professional project manager, combining and co-ordinating the various disciplines involved in the development process in the most effective way to expedite implementation. The dissipation of experience and skills gained at a national, regional as well as local level in such fields as the assessment of market potential, the arrangement of finance, the procurement of prospective occupants and the handling of delicate negotiations regarding proposed rental agreements and leasehold covenants would be a serious loss. If the future for the private developer is not to be restricted to North America, Europe and the Far and Middle East, the answer must lie in partnership.

References

1 D. Muchnick, *Urban Renewal in Liverpool – the Politics of Redevelopment,* Bell Press, 1970. Quoted in D. Frost, 'Professionalism and Bureaucracy', *Built Environment*, November 1974.
2 D. Gransby, 'A Future for the Private Developer', *Built Environment*, January 1975.

8 Partnership

To disclaim the function of planning is to disclaim social responsibility in the attainment of community goals and the amelioration of market anomalies. To deny market forces is to deny the benefits of choice and the initiatives of enterprise. Public planning and private development have disparate but complementary functions to perform; functions which in theory should surmount the defects of the other and enhance the effectiveness of both. Similar aspirations are enshrined in paragraph 57 of the White Paper on Land:

The operation of the scheme will require close co-operation between local authorities and developers, and the Government wish to see the skills and initiative of private developers contribute to the needs of the community in a positive way. Local authorities will be encouraged to involve developers in their plans, and the method of disposal should encourage developers to make a contribution towards the overall design of each scheme.[1]

Since the Community Land Act, however, simplistic or imperfect, is now not only law but also forms the basic compact or charter for future development, it is imperative that it is made to work. Recalcitrant cries for repeal are not merely peevish but actually regressive. They simply foster conditions for further uncertainty and place the prospects of the construction industry in even greater jeopardy than at present.

The need for partnership

In line with the adage that 'there is nothing new under the sun', partnership in property development between local authorities and private developers has been popularly practised since the Second World War. Fewer authorities are now prepared to dispose of freehold land and the great majority, albeit to varying degrees, seek to participate in ownership and profit sharing. As mentioned previously, many extremely successful partnership schemes conducted over the past twenty-five years have proved both socially acceptable and mutually beneficial. The very basis of New Town development has depended upon a coalition of public planning and private enterprise, and the Town Development Act has facilitated similar co-operation. Likewise, early post-war initiatives in town centre reconstruction displayed by such councils as Exeter, Sunderland, East Kilbride and especially Plymouth, bear witness to the fruits of collaborative effort. It can be fairly stated that the expectations of partnership in areas such as Telford, Central Lancashire and Milton Keynes, were inconceivable when the New Town concept was first launched, and the growing acceptance of society's fundamental right to recoup some portion of the pecuniary proceeds from the development of land created through planning decisions is now reflected across a broad consensus of moderate political opinion. Unfortunately, however, disagreements regarding the precise division of those proceeds has all too often pitched proposed partnership schemes into the tumult of political controversy, with attendant delays and disillusionment.

Substantive powers enabling local authorities to acquire, develop, manage and dispose of land have existed since the 1940s, and to some extent every municipal corporation has experience of land ownership and development. This experience ranges across the entire field of property development. There has, of course, been a long history of council housing development; local authority sponsored industrial trading estates are numerous; there has been an increasing incidence of central area comprehensive redevelopment schemes; and the physical provision of civic amenities has been very much a public sector preserve. In assessing the desirability of municipal participation in the development process, a distinction should be drawn between the functions of land ownership and an involvement in subsequent development. It will often suffice for a local authority to purchase the land, determine the future use and provide a basic infrastructure. On the other hand, it may be advantageous to participate in the actual development and retain a measure of control over the completed property. Nevertheless, the benefits of partnership to local authorities are easily identified. Such agreements permit the authority to exercise positive planning powers by initiating development; allow councils to receive a share in future development profits; enable them as landlord to exercise more effective control over the nature, use, design and management of the scheme than would otherwise be available under town planning control; provide a greater opportunity to include civic and amenity uses on valuable central area land; assist in alleviating the housing waiting list by nomination of occupants in residential partnership schemes; facilitate funding, for, whereas central government loan sanction is required for most local authority development, private sector finance is not similarly constrained; give the chance to introduce outside expertise, particularly in complex central area redevelopment situations; shed many of the financial risks inherent in property development; and more readily secure private contributions towards high infrastructure costs.

It is often argued that there is no reason why public sector authorities should not undertake total responsibility for development projects of all kinds, ensuring in this way that the full measure of betterment created as a result of planning policy, public works and social services is won back for the community. Furthermore, that local authorities should adopt a far more 'entrepreneurial, creative and opportunistic approach'[2] than hitherto. Private sector development agencies, however, are established, structured and prepared to bear risk, and, in this context, it is not always appropriate for a local authority to fulfil the role of entrepreneur and shoulder all those associated risks. Local government officers are answerable to elected representatives, who are in turn accountable to both full council and the ratepayers at large. As Powell points out,[3] shareholders in property companies and financial institutions expect their money to be at risk – ratepayers do not. It is therefore suggested, while local government should not be denied effective control over development, nor be forced to forgo substantial dividends, that in a mixed economy private enterprise should be expected to continue to play a prominent part in the process of urban development.

It should be recognized that partnership is not always a simple two-way contract, but more usually takes the form of a tripartite agreement between local authority, development agency and financial organization. Increasingly, the development agency acting on behalf of the financial organization is one of the leading national firms of chartered surveyors, operating in a project management capacity. It can therefore be seen that future developments will be conducted by consortia of local authorities, property development companies and financial institutions, or combinations thereof, with professional property and development consultants called in as required. With circumstances predictably dictating cases, the individual format of partnership agreements is bound to vary, but differing degrees of accountability will inevitably affect the respective responsibilities. As previously intimated, for example, the public accountability of local authorities, and their potential conflicts of interest, should preclude them from assuming sole responsibility for development, except in the most risk-free situations. A different, but nevertheless conscious, accountability on the part of financial institutions to their pensioners and policyholders again restricts the degree of allowable risk and produces a preference for long-term relatively secure investment propositions in circumstances where they are obliged to act almost alone. The property development company only answers to its shareholders whose initial investment decisions were, in all probability, motivated by the prospects of profitability engendered in risk situations. It can, therefore, be contended that in complex high-risk conditions, such as those encountered in large-scale commercial development, the respective responsibilities should be apportioned according to the risk-bearing capacities of the parties concerned. It is appropriate, for example, that the local authority should retain a prior interest in the land with a possible share in future benefits depending upon success; that a funding institution should possess a substantial long-term leasehold interest, again with prospects of a future share in profits; and that the riskiest elements of the scheme should be borne by the development company responsible for conception, design, implementation and marketing of the project, which could then expect the incentive of commensurate short-term, top-slice rewards. It has also been put forward that where partnership agreements have been entered into between public and private organizations, all parties should share the financial burden of their joint decisions in respect of both profit and loss.[4]

Methods of partnership

In examining the potential opportunities for employing partnership schemes between local authorities and private enterprise to carry out major housing development in the South East, the Department of the Environment commissioned, in 1972, a working party to consider the possible methods and background issues of partnership.[5] Although the report confined itself to residential development, many of the recommendations apply equally to commercial development, and a number of principal partnership arrangements can be identified.

Firstly, *agreements made under Section 52* of the Town and Country

Planning Act 1971, which enable a local authority to enter into covenants with persons having an interest in land for the purpose of restricting or regulating the development or use of that land, either permanently or for a limited period. Roughly similar provisions, but requiring ministerial consent, were contained in planning Acts as early as 1944. Such agreements should be made before the grant of planning permission and might include covenants regarding a developer's financial contribution to infrastructure costs, the transfer of land for civic amenities, the phasing of development or the provision of particular services or facilities. Before 1974, the main problem with this method was that only restrictive covenants, and not the positive part of agreements, were enforceable against successors in title, although specific authority could always be obtained by Private Act of Parliament. It is perhaps surprising that by 1974, only thirty-seven authorities had availed themselves of this special facility. Section 126 of the 1974 Housing Act now gives local authorities certain powers to make transactions under seal in respect of their housing functions, to enforce positive covenants against third parties. Confusion still reigns, however, regarding the legal difficulties surrounding the use of planning agreements, and it has been suggested that the remaining anachronistic distinctions between positive and negative covenants should be abolished.[6] In any event, such agreements, which can be said to use private procedures to achieve public objectives, are essentially voluntary in nature; must not purport to make development contingent upon contributions in cash or in kind if the development would otherwise be reasonable; are rarely appropriate where large-scale development is countenanced or where a great number of ownerships are involved unless perhaps the local authority owns certain key sites; and arguably subvert the function of conditional planning permission which might be more usefully extended.

The second method is the formation of *trusts for sale* or *syndicates*. Under the former arrangement, local authorities and landowners would appoint trustees to sell sites for development in accordance with an acceptable plan and subject to agreed contributions towards infrastructure, and under the latter a designated development area would be co-operatively assembled and disposed of for development by landowners with or without local authority participation, but employing relevant Section 52 agreements in respect of local services, amenity land, layout, design and programming. One of the main problems with such transactions is that they require virtually unanimous agreement among all the parties concerned, and at present the schemes usually amount to a substantial departure to the approved development plan, and it is not unknown for the Department of the Environment to refuse planning permission at inquiry. The advantages to the local authority, however, are said to be that no further legislative powers are required to implement the scheme, and much of the detailed work is shared between the parties; those to the owners are said to include certain kinds of tax avoidance, and that local knowledge and commitment reduce delay.

A third, and probably more significant, method is *comprehensive land assembly by local authorities* whereby authorities acquire all relevant development land in the first instance, retain those sites required for their own civic development projects, and dispose to other public bodies or private developers remaining sites as appropriate. In many ways, the wide application of such a procedure would require a fundamental change in policy on the part of most local authorities, both in adopting a more adventurous attitude to land assembly and in establishing a closer rapport with development agencies. The obvious drawback to this approach is that until the second appointed day envisaged in the Community Land Act, the availability of sufficient capital funds is likely to be severely restricted. In due course, it is hoped that a rolling programme of acquisition, development and disposal will create a self-financing system of advance land assembly.

Fourthly, although currently no general statutory powers exist, it is possible to obtain special powers by Private Act of Parliament to form a *joint company*. This could be variously set up with landowners, developers, financial institutions or construction companies, or a combination thereof. The joint company concept is a highly sophisticated development organization and consequently when the number of prospective partners is large, the procedure becomes complex and less attractive. In other situations, however, it can provide an extremely efficient machinery for development, equity sharing and, because the joint operations can be separated for accounting purposes, thereby avoiding ministerial loan sanction, funding. One proviso should be that if the negotiated funding facility has to be supported by local authority collateral the council will be ultimately liable to raise loans in the normal way in the event of the company failing to meet its obligations. An elementary example of such an approach is the formation of a joint equity sharing company between the local authority and landowners where individual owners are guaranteed a share in the equity arising from the subsequent development of land. This could be so structured as either to provide landowners with a dividend share in the company or to permit the local authority to form a company in its own right and guarantee owners a future equity participation without distributing company shares. Both arrangements could also include an initial part capital payment to the landowners. A recent instance of such an arrangement was the formation by special Act of Parliament in 1971 of the Buckingham Borough Development Company Ltd. A detailed description of the history and structure of the company is available elsewhere,[7] but essentially the company was set up by the county council and the borough council to assemble, service and develop land for future town expansion. It was initially financed by county council short-term loans secured by debentures issued against the company and overdraft facilities guaranteed by the county. It is envisaged that further capital will be raised from private sources as required. An agreement in principle was reached between the company and the owners of land identified for future development whereby, in general, the owners were paid £500 per acre for five-year options to purchase and guaranteed a further £3500 per acre when the options were taken up. After development or disposition a further payment would become due comprising 75 per cent of the net development profit depending on the price received for the land. The remaining 25 per cent would go to the company who could use it to improve local facilities. The main advantages to the landowners are the privileged tax position enjoyed from a straight sale to the local authority and the opportunity of a relatively riskless investment. The success of such partnership schemes obviously relies heavily upon achieving a majority agreement, and it can be argued that the private share of the development 'spoils' is unacceptably disproportionate in order to ensure co-operation.

Naturally, the range and variety of partnership schemes are by no means exclusive but another potentially popular approach is the setting up of joint companies with developers. These arrangements are not unlike those entered into in many town centre redevelopment schemes in the past where comprehensive land assembly occurs as a prelude to joint development, so that the success of the project is not contingent upon the pattern or attitudes of prevailing ownership. A basic model to effect this policy can be distinguished involving the establishment of a joint co-ordinating agency or company comprising the county and district authorities concerned who would be charged with the responsibility of promoting land assembly in key areas, negotiating with developers and setting up individual joint companies to undertake the actual development. The initial capital for the joint company would be provided entirely from the private sector either by the developers themselves or more probably in collaboration with a financial institution. A share subscription would determine the respective proportions of equity participation with some share capital going to the joint agency in return for the provision of services and some possibly being given to the original landowners. The share capital enjoyed by the joint agency would not necessarily attract a dividend because their returns might well take the form of a conveyance of land for community facilities on favourable terms or a direct payment for services. An example of such an agreement, albeit on a relatively small scale, can be seen in Norwich, where the local authority purchased a three-acre central area site consisting of derelict land but potentially of high amenity value, as well as a group of buildings of special architectural and historic interest.[8] Rejecting the usual long-leasehold partnership basis, which tends to delegate too much estate control and ties up long-term capital funds, the council formed a joint company called Colegate Developments Ltd with local builders who will share equally in all future profits once the original cost of the land has been recouped. Along similar lines, Manchester have formed a limited liability corporation comprehensively to redevelop a large central area site with finance being provided by an insurance company, a property developer and public subscription, with the corporation retaining 25 per cent of eventual profits. To facilitate the building-up of their land bank another authority, Hampshire, have entered into an agreement with merchant bankers, Hill Samuel, under which land worth £11 million has been assembled on options with a 'rolled-up' or 'warehoused' fixed rate of interest over a five- to nine-year period. The notion of *development consultancy* as a method of partnership has been taken a step further by an organization called LOGOS (Local Government Services) which is made up of three specialist firms with experience in economic planning, finance and marketing services who offer local authorities urban development services on a consultancy fee basis.

Despite the obvious benefits conferred by partnership between public and private sectors, a number of problematical issues can be discerned. Firstly, certain problems might arise in respect of the accountability of public funds where an authority is financially involved in company trading transactions, although it is argued that normal auditing procedures should be sufficient safeguard. Secondly, the possibility arises of conflicts of interest mentioned in Chapter 5 that might emerge between the responsibility for formulating and implementing public planning policy and the involvement in entrepreneurial development activity. Again it has been suggested that such a situation need not arise so long as the local authority land assembly and disposition takes place within the context of an approved statutory framework.[9] Thirdly, that compulsory, acquisition by local authorities in exisitng urban areas, even existing use value, could prove so prohibitive that with present loan allocations the burden must be borne by private institutions with a consequent inflation in cost as landowners recognize the strength of their protected bargaining position and bid up the price. Nevertheless, whatever the drawbacks, the potentialities of partnership are enormous so long as an effective planning framework can be evolved and a more co-operative basis established.

The partnership process

It bears repetition to recall that a legislative framework enabling partnership between public and private sectors has existed since the 1944 Town and Country Planning Act. This attempted to tackle the comprehensive redevelopment of blitzed and blighted areas caused by the Second World War and was subsequently extended to areas of bad layout and obsolete development, so that over the intervening period, a number of alternative courses of co-operative action have emerged. The majority of these have involved the local authority in land assembly, usually through the exercise of compulsory purchase powers, the carrying out of necessary infrastructure works, and the subsequent disposal of land on a long ground lease to a private development agency. Initially, the ground lease was for ninety-nine years at a fixed rent, but through the 1950s periodic ground rent reviews at approximately twenty-five-year intervals either to open market value or to an agreed proportion of the total rack rent were included, and through time these have been reduced to fourteen-, and more recently seven-year intervals and even less, while the term has often been extended to 125 years to match the demands of the financial institutions who theoretically allow for reconstruction during the lease period. Since the middle 1960s, more sophisticated forms of partnership have evolved to account for local authority limitations in the financing of land assembly and to permit greater municipal participation in development profits. In consequence, it is impossible authoritatively to describe a particular process of partnership which varies from site to site, from authority to authority and from use to use, but the following outline gives an indication of some of the basic elements.

The principal steps in the process of development through partnership are naturally analogous to those set out in the preceding chapter describing the private sector development process. The main differences in the early stages where a local authority is involved are that during *site identification*, local demand should reflect community need as well as profitability; *preliminary appraisal* will take greater account of prevailing planning policies and public works programmes for the area; much more information will be available for the preparation of an *outline programme* and a *detailed investigation*; and the *development decision* will involve public participation and be determined by elected representatives in addition to private development agencies. The procedures for *site assembly* will vary according to the party taking the initiative for development, because private initiatives can be covert and free from statutory procedure, whereas public initiatives must be publicized and subjected to the various statutory procedures relating to such obligations as consultation, service of compulsory purchase notices and orders, highway closure and inquiries. Currently such initiatives are taken separately by public authorities or private agencies and partnership occurs comparatively late in the process. It is evident that under the Community Land Act, partnership schemes will play a more prominent role in urban development and will require setting-up at the earliest possible stage in the process, which automatically implies a statutory adherence to public procedures for acquisition.

In circumstances where the scheme is initially a local authority sponsored development, an additional stage will occur where the authority is faced with a *choice of development agency*. This will entail deciding whether to undertake the development themselves, in which case no partnership takes place, or to enter into an agreement with a development agency, be it a property company, financial institution or a construction firm. The selection of the agency is conducted in one of four ways:[10] by architectural competition between four to six developers, ideally reflecting the span of different agencies such as an institution, a builder and a property company, and based on a planning and development brief prepared by the local authority; by financial competition based upon a similar brief;

by a combination of both architectural and financial competition; or by a negotiation with a preferred developer selected from a short list. It is essential in the first three methods that imponderable aspects of both design and finance are reduced to a minimum, because the cost to private firms of indulging in such competitions is high and the results uncertain. For this reason, tendering procedures along the lines described have now become less popular over the past few years and many authorities have opted to negotiate with a particular developer, a method which has the added advantage of allowing the developer to operate in close collaboration with the authority from the inception of the scheme, thereby harmonizing the mutual skills of public and private processes and tackling social, cultural and environmental problems against a continuing test of economic feasibility.

Over the past ten years, conventional partnership schemes have usually provided for an arrangement whereby the local authority, having assembled the land, leases the site to a developer for 99 or 125 years on an initial ground rent as described above, but in addition negotiates for itself a pre-arranged share in any future increases in rental profit which may be assessed annually or at longer intervals. It is also a common feature of partnership, particularly in town centre redevelopment, that the developer undertakes site acquisition and assembly, and that the price paid for the land is calculated on the basis of compensation applicable to Comprehensive Development Areas, with the local authority being prepared selectively to exercise reserve powers of compulsory purchase in circumstances where the developing company finds it impossible to effect acquisition by agreement.

The remaining stages in the process surrounding the setting up of the professional team, pre-contract and contract negotiation, design, construction and marketing can be collectively grouped together as the *project management* stage. Although the Community Land Act focusses the attention of local authorities upon the desirability of developing land themselves, it is inevitable, especially in large-scale complex development situations, that other external agencies in the financial, development and construction fields will be involved, and that the overall management of the project will also be shared. In the past most authorities, possessing limited commercial experience, have been prepared to delegate the function of project management in intricate commercial development situations to private enterprise. It is possible that such a trusting disposition will be tempered in the future by a growing desire to exercise greater control over the entire process, with the result that the respective roles will be even more difficult to define.

Financial arrangements

In the final analysis, the kernel of the problem lies in finance. Not merely the availability of development funds, but also the distribution of profits. If continuity of urban development and improvement is to be assured, a free flow of funds must be maintained from both public and private sectors, for traditionally local authorities have financed development by direct borrowing, or from private sources through the medium of a third party, or by a combination of both. Direct borrowing from the Public Works Loan Board or from the capital or money markets is subject to statutory authorization either by way of local enabling Acts relating to the financing of specific works, or through the need to obtain consent from a 'sanctioning authority', which in the case of land acquisition prior to partnership is the Secretary of State for the Department of the Environment. Municipal borrowing is further classified for purposes of control into two major divisions – *key sector* expenditure which relates to the provision of those services and facilities such as housing, education, principal roads, water supply and major sewerage works which are determined at a national level; and expenditure for *locally determined schemes* which is provided in the form of a block allocation to local authorities and includes a degree of financial support for advance land assembly. The former is particularly susceptible to changes in national economic policy, and it has been argued[11] that in respect of the latter, the lack of prior consultation between central and local government, the inadequate budgetary time-scale and the inherent inflexibility of the system has resulted in a slowing down in the pace of development and redevelopment and consequently driven local authorities into the arms of developers. As the Department of the Environment report on partnership schemes indicates, several alternative arrangements for financing land assembly which do not count against their current loan sanction allocations are available to local authorities. These include the use of capital receipts, the acquisition and disposal of land within a financial year and the purchase of land from revenue money or from capital funds. They may also apply to the Secretary of State for an individual allocation from the special 'large projects pool' which is built-up by retaining a percentage from the locally determined schemes account.

The proportion of private funds which has become available to local authorities as a result of direct and indirect borrowing from the capital and money markets has seriously diminished over the past few years, a tendency which detracts from the effective partnership role of local authorities, because if more funds became available for the public assembly and servicing of development land, the implicit powers of ownership would reduce the need for authorities to participate in the final stages of development which could properly be left to private enterprise. Assuming, however, that a local authority has managed to assemble land for prospective development, it is imperative that the best possible partnership agreement is transacted, the highest possible ground rent obtained for the site and the best future participation in profits negotiated. The following simple example demonstrates the basic rationale underlying the financial arrangements conducted between local authority and developer. The example is based upon a development scheme with construction costs of £2·4 million, a probable rental level of £400 000 per annum, a 10 per cent cost of finance and an acceptable developer's profit based upon $2\frac{1}{2}$ per cent of total cost, the ground rent is calculated as follows:

Estimated current rental value		£400 000 p.a.
Less: Loan repayments at 10% on £2·4 million	£240 000 p.a.	
Annual return at $2\frac{1}{2}$% on £2·4 million	£ 60 000 p.a.	£300 000 p.a.
Ground rent payable to local authority		£100 000 p.a.

It is possible that the local authority might seek an initial capital payment, say £400 000, in the form of a premium in return for receiving a reduced rent and the calculation would be amended as in the first table opposite.

Furthermore, many partnership arrangements are designed so that the local authority as freeholder can increase its ground rent following the completion of the development in circumstances where actual rents achieved exceed estimated rental levels. Such a device

Estimated current rental value		£400 000 p.a.
Less:		
Loan repayments at 10% on £2·4 million	£240 000 p.a.	
Loan repayments at 10% on £400 000	£ 40 000 p.a.	
Annual return at 2½% on £2·8 million	£ 70 000 p.a.	£350 000 p.a.
Ground rent payable to local authority after payment of premium	£400 000	£ 50 000 p.a.

is known as a 'participation' clause, whereby the freeholder shares
in the increased rental value according to an agreed percentage, and
should be distinguished from rent reviews, which follow in the years
to come and are often established at the participation rate. Using
the same figures as before, but assuming that the actual rack rents
achieved total £600 000 per annum, and no premium is required,
the calculation of participation is conducted as shown below:

Estimated rental value		£400 000 p.a.
Negotiated initial ground rental payable to local authority		£100 000 p.a.
Local authority initial equity	$\frac{£100\,000}{£400\,000} \times 100 =$	25%
Actual rents achieved after completion of development		£600 000 p.a.
Agreed local authority share in increased rental value	say 50%	
Actual rental value	£600 000 p.a.	
Estimated rental value	£400 000 p.a.	
Increased equity	£200 000 p.a.	
Local authority share at 50% =	£100 000 p.a.	
Revised ground rent = £100 000 p.a. + £100 000 p.a. = £200 000 p.a.		
Equity share to local authority at future reviews	$\frac{£200\,000 \times 100}{£600\,000} =$	£33·3%

A further refinement often employed in assessing the respective equities of participation between local authority and development agency is the inclusion of a *yield protection* clause, whereby the developer is guaranteed an agreed bottom-slice yield on the cost of the development before the local authority receive a participatory increase in ground rent. Assuming the agreed yield protection is 15 per cent, the calculation is as follows.:

Actual rents achieved after completion of development		£600 000 p.a.
Less: Initial ground rent	£100 000 p.a.	
15% Yield protection on £2·4 million	£360 000 p.a.	£460 000 p.a.
	Increased equity	£140 000 p.a.
	50%	£ 70 000 p.a.
Actual rent achieved after completion of development		£600 000 p.a.
Less: Initial ground rent	£100 000 p.a.	
15% Yield protection on £2·4 million	£360 000 p.a.	£460 000 p.a.
Increased shared equity		£140 000 p.a.
Revised ground rent=£100 000+£70 000 p.a.=		£170 000 p.a.
Equity share to local authority at future reviews	$\dfrac{£170\,000 \times 100}{£600\,000} =$	28·3%

The future prospects

The almost inevitable concomitant of exploring the underlying problems of propitiating divergent political opinion regarding community created land values is a realization that the recondite nature of proposals for land tenure reform, operating within concurrent systems of development and planning, virtually precludes the devising of a single policy solution that is both theoretically sound and at the same time capable of ready implementation. The complexity of underlying determinants tends to result in criteria for a solution which are mutually incompatible, for permanence is at odds with political acceptability, public authority controls vie with private sector interests, and long-term estate management policies clash with short-term development expediency. As Richardson asserts: 'Panaceas and "only solutions" have a poor track record.'[12]

In a highly complex urban and industrialized society, one, furthermore, which functions as a mixed economy where the pressures upon land and resulting scarcities create innumerable social problems, it is incumbent upon government to contrive an array of measures in the short run designed to ameliorate the dilemma of land values. Some of these measures will attempt to remedy the fiscal aspects of betterment and worsenment, others will seek to rectify the defects in the planning process caused by inflationary land value spirals and supply constraints. The range and variety of measures should be designed in such a way as to permit either the control or stimulation of development according to local conditions, to appeal to a wide spectrum of political opinion, to aid regional development, to promote growth areas, and to be suitable for particular planning purposes such as New Town development, central area schemes, renewal of twilight housing zones, and the establishment of industrial estates.

This varied and flexible approach does not deny the long-term introduction of more progressive solutions, nor does it necessarily imply a perpetuation of recent 'ad-hocery'. It should consist of a set of related and integrated policies, agencies, controls and standards all operating within an overall framework. The framework itself is bound to have certain national political connotations, not to mention a changing social and economic perspective, but it is vital, as previously intimated, that it should be constructed upon an understanding of the special nature of land, the intricate form of the market in rights over land, and the complicated mechanism driving the forces which direct the performance of the development process and the institutions responsible for its actions.

In attempting to ensure continuity of implementation within such a framework, one of the most attractive solutions is the formation of *public development companies*. Taking the proposals for the establishment of a single, national public development company or agency, which have been variously advanced in a number of quarters over the past few years,[13] a little further, it is suggested that the setting-up of a series of publicly orientated companies would greatly facilitate the operation of the Community Land Act. The French have successfully experimented with similar bodies both in terms of their *sociétés d'économie mixte*[14] and the more recent creation of specific agencies such as the *Agence Foncière et Technique de la Région Parisienne* (AFTRP) and the *Etablissement Public Basse-Sevrie* (EPBS).[15] Appropriate organizations for this country would have a company structure whose shareholders would include local authorities, financial institutions and private investors, and could be regionally based. They would purchase land at market values but ahead of development and redevelopment programmes, and would be exempt from Development Land Tax. Operating in this way, they would not only internalize community created values, but also assist in co-ordinating planning policy. Furthermore, they could make available to local authorities a range of tenures such as site leaseholds, co-operatives, associations and occasionally, where political circumstances dictated, freehold for owner occupation. The great strength of these companies is that in acting as a catalyst for land assembly and development, they could permit a variety of local permutations according to prevailing political conditions and changing socio-economic exigencies. The level of their activity and the degree of their involvement would eventually relate directly to their proven worth, because they would continue to rely upon the inflow of investment funds from satisfied shareholders.

Whatever the prospects are for the future, and whoever may be the agents of implementation, the critical observations made throughout this book are not to deny some of the benefits to be derived from public ownership and development partnership, but are made to stress that such a policy is not on its own enough. It does not guarantee efficiency; it does not automatically produce better, or even adequate, development; extra planning, intervention and control are not necessarily synonymous with effective urban administration. Moreover, the evidence upon which policies are formulated and solutions advanced is scant and superficial. A great deal more research requires to be undertaken on such issues as gauging the impact in terms of the redistribution of land values of a whole range of planning policies, investigating the social and economic results of various forms of landowner-planner-developer-builder relationships, formulating the most efficient means of management policy and practice, examining the most appropriate arrangements for effectively co-ordinating public sector involvement in urban development, and most important of all, assembling data on the relationship between land development costs and land value revenues in order to determine the financial viability of respective systems. In this way, any acceptable solutions to the abstruse dilemma of betterment and worsenment and the complementary formulation of an effective land policy should be designed in such a way as to preserve the beneficial attributes of the development process while seeking to correct its failings and redress its worst anomalies. The mutual recriminations of planning and development, though relentless, are fruitless and futile.

References

1 Department of the Environment, *Land*, Cmnd. 5730, HMSO, 1975.
2 N. Falk, 'The Community as Developer', *Built Environment*, April 1974.
3 G. Powell, 'Local Authority Participation in the Profits of Local Property Developments and the Disposal of Land by Local Authorities', *Chartered Survey: Urban Quarterly*, vol. 1, no. 3, 1974.
4 RICS, Memorandum of Evidence to the Advisory Group on Commercial Property Development, *Chartered Surveyor*, August/September 1975.
5 Department of the Environment, *Report of the Working Party on Local Authority/Private Enterprise Partnership Schemes*, HMSO, 1972.
6 M. Grant, 'Planning by Agreement', *Journal of Planning and Environment Law*, September 1975.
7 Department of the Environment, 1972, *op. cit.*
8 *ibid.*
9 *ibid.*
10 RICS, *op. cit.*
11 R. Green, 'The Role of Private Finance in Local Government Development, with Special Reference to Land Banks', *Paper to the Town and Country Planning Association Conference*, July 1974.
12 H. Richardson, 'On Public Ownership', *New Society*, 28 June 1973.
13 See for example:
   R. Barras, *et al.*, 'Planning and the Public Ownership of Land', *New Society*, 21 June 1973.
   M. Ash, 'Development Agencies and the Community Land Bill', *Estates Gazette*, 14 June 1975.
14 Ash, *ibid.*
15 J. Lacaze, *The Role of the French New Towns in Regional Development and Regional Life*, Report to the 6th Congress of the International Council of Regional Economics, May 1972.

Subject Index

Author Index